What people are saying about
Woman to Woman Wisdom: Inspiration for Real Life

"*Woman to Woman Wisdom* had [...] active, these inspirational stories show how to be defined from within. So important in today's times. The wisdom imparted helps me live with intention. I will be giving this beautiful book as a gift to ALL my friends!"

—**Naomi Judd,** Grammy Award-winning singer/songwriter

"This profound *Woman to Woman Wisdom* is a 'must have' book for legions of women. It is a tender work … and a serious one."

—**Maya Angelou,** Poet, Playwright, Author

"I have been fortunate in my life to be surrounded by many wise women— my mother, Jimmy's mother Miss Lillian, and many others—and to benefit from their guidance and encouragement. There is no substitute for 'woman to woman' wisdom that is shared from the heart and grounded in God's messages. Everyone seeking direction and support for life's challenges can gain insight from the selected Scriptures and the personal experiences of the three outstanding women in this truly lovely, inspirational book."

—**Rosalynn Carter,** former First Lady of Georgia and the United States

"There is nothing more important than knowing that my girlfriends are always there when I need them. In *Woman to Woman Wisdom*, I can experience the love of God through girlfriend talk."

—**Janet Huckabee,** First Lady, Arkansas

"This lovely book is filled with thoughtful ideas for how to tune in to God's presence and wisdom."

—**Gail Sheehy,** Author, *Passages*

"This is a beautiful, faith-based book. Simply lovely. And inspired."
—**Jennifer Read Hawthorne,** Coauthor, *Chicken Soup for the Woman's Soul*

"*Woman to Woman Wisdom: Inspiration for Real Life,* will motivate, inspire and uplift you. It will give you a boost when you are low, a lift when you are down and a thrust when you think you're already at the top. Read a little at a time. Reflect on the words and allow the divine wisdom within the pages to direct your steps."

—**Dr. Robert A. Schuller,** Crystal Cathedral

"This book, *Woman to Woman Wisdom,* is so powerful for women. Thank you Bettie, Linda and Donna for giving us this warm, witty, wise and wonderful book."

—**Cathy Keating,** former First Lady, Oklahoma

"These beautiful devotionals provide every woman with positive, uplifting and practical Christian insights. Simply a heartwarming and assuring book."

—**Dorothy Benham,** wife, mother, singer,
businesswoman, Miss America 1977

"Through the stories in this simply beautiful book, Bettie Youngs, Linda Caldwell Fuller and Donna Schuller identify the all-important role of women. May God bless this important book."

—**Mel Cheatham,** Author, *Make a Difference: Responding to God's Call to Love the World;* Billy Graham Evangelistic Association board of directors

"Straight from the heart—a book for women, about things important to women. I was entranced."

—**Stephanie Woodend,** Prison Fellowship Ministries

"Men can learn a lot from the really special insights of women. My wife and I will be sharing *Woman to Woman Wisdom: Inspiration for Real Life* with our daughters and other close friends."

—**Ron Glosser,** Vice-Chairman, Guideposts, Inc.

"These daily devotions are a wonderful spiritual resource for nurturing an honest relationship with the Lord in the midst of life's complex realities."

—**Richard J. Mouw,** President and professor of
Christian Philosophy, Fuller Seminary

"This is a book of wise insights and warm-hearted responses to life's potpourri of experiences by three remarkable women. . . . a truly lovely book."

—**Dr. Robert H. and Arvella Schuller**

"What an awe-inspiring collection of shared stories, thoughts and prayers that serve to remind us that our God is an awesome God."

—**Calina Cook-Burns,** Vice-President of CBuJ Entertainment; President of Go Grrrl Records; Vice-President of The Lymphatic Research Foundation

"This book will inspire your heart, challenge your mind, touch your funny bone and help women everywhere navigate the wonders and challenges along the road of life!"

—**Don and Cheryl Barber,** Hosts of *Good News TV*

"My friends Bettie, Linda and Donna have written this book to encourage you as you live out the ups and downs of your life story. Together we can listen . . . love . . . and let ourselves be loved by the great God who is always there."

—**Linda LeSourd Lader,** Cofounder, Renaissance Weekend

"This book has truly changed my outlook on the importance of the many hats I wear, and the roles for which I shoulder responsibility."

—**Jamie Hardwick,** Program Executive, Girl Scouts of Appleseed Ridge

"Superb!"

—**Bob Edgar,** National Council of Churches USA

"What makes women so supremely wise is that we KNOW that *all* experiences have 'Spirit' written *into* them. Such is the spirit you will find within each page of this deeply truth-filled book."

—**Jennifer Youngs,** Coauthor, *Taste Berries for Teens* series, and Author, *Feeling Great, Looking Hot and Loving Yourself: Health, Fitness & Beauty for Teens*

"Any book with the words 'wisdom' and 'inspiration' in the title is making a bold claim. In this case, the claim is well-justified."

—**Mark Atteberry,** Author, *The Samson Syndrome* and *The Caleb Quest*

"Open your heart and let this book in. You will be better for it. You will be touched."

—**Michelle Thomas,** St. Rita's Hospital, Ohio

"Poetic and strong, this soul-filled book will inspire women of all generations with heart-warming experiences of love, life and friendships shared."

—**Traci Shuman,** *Star Beacon News*

"This beautiful book offers great insight into what makes life meaningful."

—**Jerry Freed,** former Publisher, Westminster/John Knox Press

"*Woman to Woman Wisdom* really puts the reader in touch with God's deep, unconditional love for each of us."

—**Sister Mary Agnes Spampinato,** CSJ, Baden, PA

"*Woman to Woman Wisdom* nurtures, challenges and encourages the reader toward fulfillment while continuing to focus her on God, the source of all power and sustenance."

—**Rev. Paul B. Raushenbush,** Princeton University, Office of Religious Life

"I pray that each woman who reads this book finds her wholeness and fulfillment in the love of God that is so openly shared by these wise women."

—**Marilyn White,** Publisher, *Precious Times*

"A divinely inspired work, one that has drawn me closer to my Heavenly Father. What a glorious message to share with other 'sisters'!"

—**Susan M. Heim,** former Senior Editor, Health Communications, Inc. and Faith Communications, Inc.

"In *Woman to Woman Wisdom,* these three amazing authors share their own stories of life lived for the ultimate purpose of serving each other—and serving God. These devotionals and prayers will inspire you to become all that God has called you to be."

—**Michael Popkin, Ph.D.,** President and founder, Active Parenting Publishers

"Thanks to the loving words in this book, we are given a broader expression of experiences and an understanding of our paths."

—**Betty Blair,** Marketing & Media, Del Mar Thoroughbred Racing Club

"Like the warmth of a mother's hug, *Woman to Woman Wisdom* will lead your heart to joy and peace!"

—**Brittany Waggoner,** Author of *Prayers for When You're Mad, Sad or Just Totally Confused*

"*Woman to Woman Wisdom* is a testament to the power and strength of both faith and the support of fellow women."

—**Katherine Essig Edgewood,** Senior high educator, Ohio

"It was not my plan to stay up so late and read *Woman To Woman Wisdom*— but rather God's plan. It is authored by three dynamic women that combine their vast experiences and love of God's word into a blueprint for dealing with the challenges of life."

—**John St. Augustine,** Power!Talk Radio

"Enjoy and savor every word in this divinely inspired book."

—**Barbara Metzler,** Author of *The Power of Purpose*

"With an open heart and a gentle touch, this wonderful collection of uplifting messages and inspiring prayers will appeal to faithful women of every denomination. Just beautiful!"

—**Arielle Ford,** The Spiritual Cinema Circle

"*Woman to Woman Wisdom* delivers invaluable truths for our spirit. A must for your bedside stand."

—**Donna Hartley,** Speaker and Author, *Fire Up Your Life!*

"After reading *Woman to Woman Wisdom*, I feel as if I've just had coffee with my three closest friends!"

—**Marla Martenson,** Actress, *What Women Want*

"This is a book for your heart. May it enrich your life as it has mine."

—**Lauren Gartland,** President, Building Champions

"This divine book provides wonderful insights, both into the light of the remarkable women who have written it and into the heart of the God they connect us to."

—**Dr. Christine Sine,** former Medical Director, Mercy Ships

"Savor these words. They're special, and wise, in many ways."

—**Peggy Campolo,** Author and Speaker

"This uplifting collection of devotionals offers glimpses into the lives of three exemplary women who share with us their wisdom of life's lessons learned."

—**Janet Spier,** retired educator, founder,
Coachella Valley Habitat for Humanity

"Reading *Woman to Woman Wisdom* brings encouragement, inspiration and a positive focus for the day."

—**Wilma C. Caldwell,** ninety-two-year-old mother of Linda C. Fuller

"A stunning collection of inspirational stories."

—**Wanda Urbanska,** Author, *Nothing's Too Small to Make a Difference;*
host, *Simple Living with Wanda Urbanska*

"Written with a mighty pen, these power-filled stories, strikingly bold and yet tender, will forever stop your being uncertain of 'who' you are."

—Vanessa L. Vega, M.S., Educator, Coauthor, *All Poetry for Teens*

"This is a 'must-read' for all women desiring a deeper understanding as to the meaning of life and increasing compassion for all of our varied and sometimes troubling journeys through life."

—Nancy Chappie, Founding president, Travel University International

"Thank you, God, for giving Donna, Bettie and Linda the heart and wisdom to speak so eloquently to other women. This book is truly inspiring."

—Lanelle Titello, Donna Schuller's mother

"I believe that many, many lives will be touched and inspired by the faith-walked so eloquently told in this heartfelt book."

—Rev. Ted Nace, Peale Center for Christian Living, a Division of Guidepost

"While reading *Woman to Woman Wisdom*, I felt as though I could sit and talk with each of these women on so many of the experiences written about. I loved the reminder that God is always at my side, and that the solutions are always the best ones when we let Spirit rule our hearts."

—Dianne York-Goldman, Author of *You Glow Girl* and President, La Jolla Spa MD

"*Woman to Woman Wisdom* is sure to warm the heart and touch the soul of any woman who reads it."

—Debbie Thurman, Sheer Faith Ministries, Coauthor, *A Teen's Guide to Christian Living: Practical Answers to Tough Questions About God and Faith*

"This book is a *must* read for every woman."

—National League of American Pen Women, Inc., La Jolla Branch

woman
to woman
wisdom

Inspiration for REAL Life

Bettie B. Youngs, Ph.D, Ed.D.

Linda C. Fuller

Donna M. Schuller, C.N.C.

NELSON BOOKS
A Division of Thomas Nelson Publishers
Since 1798

www.thomasnelson.com

Published in Nashville, Tennessee, by Thomas Nelson, Inc.

Nelson Books titles may be purchased in bulk for educational, business, fund-raising, or sales promotional use. For information, please e-mail SpecialMarkets@ThomasNelson.com.

Unless otherwise noted, Scripture quotations are taken from the HOLY BIBLE, NEW INTERNATIONAL VERSION®. Copyright © 1973, 1978, 1984 by International Bible Society. Used by permission of Zondervan Bible Publishing House. All rights reserved.

The "NIV" and "New International Version" trademarks are registered in the United States Patent and Trademark Office by International Bible Society. Use of either trademark requires the permission of International Bible Society.

Scripture quotations noted KJV are from The Holy Bible, KING JAMES VERSION.

Scripture quotations marked CEV are from THE CONTEMPORARY ENGLISH VERSION of the Bible. Copyright © 1991, 1995 by the American Bible Society. Used by permission.

Scripture quotations noted *The Message* are from *The Message: The New Testament in Contemporary English,* by Eugene H. Peterson. Copyright © 1993, 1994, 1995, 1996, 2000. Used by permission of NavPress Publishing Group. All rights reserved.

Scripture quotations noted NASB are taken from THE NEW AMERICAN STANDARD BIBLE ®. Copyright © The Lockman Foundation 1960, 1962, 1963, 1968, 1971, 1972, 1973, 1975, 1977. Used by permission. (www.Lockman.org)

Library of Congress Cataloging-in-Publication Data

Youngs, Bettie B.
  Woman to woman wisdom : inspiration for real life / Bettie B. Youngs, Linda C. Fuller, Donna M. Schuller.
      p. cm.
  ISBN 0-7852-1261-2 (pbk.)
  1. Women—Prayer-books and devotions—English. 2. Women—Religious life. I. Fuller, Linda, 1941– II. Schuller, Donna. III. Title.
  BV4844.Y68 2005
  242'.643—dc22   2005007061

Printed in the United States of America
1 2 3 4 5 6 RRD 07 08 06 05

I will give you a wise and discerning heart,
so that there will never have been anyone like you,
nor will there ever be.

(1 Kings 3:12)

Contents

Foreword

An old Eastern saying has always been true: Women do hold up half of the sky. And we've been doing it since the beginning of time. Before women gained legal rights to own property, enter business and the professions, vote, and hold church office, our dear mothers and grandmothers were holding up their share in the ways open to them. They loved, encouraged and counseled. They managed homes, raised children, worked side-by-side with their husbands, yet still found the strength and opportunity to create hospitals, orphanages, and urban missions to fill the most pressing human needs. And they accomplished this *woman-to-woman:* Each generation of women has passed along to other women the wisdom they gained to best help humanity.

We all know women who have a lot to teach us about service to humanity. For me, it was my mother. Her influence in my life was clearly powerful. We were a military family and moved about, but always she created a sense of home, instilled the importance of meaning, purpose, and direction, and through her strong, committed, and fearless leadership, she demonstrated the presence of the Lord wherever we lived. Certainly, she was a shining example of the Christian life.

Today, there are more opportunities than ever for a woman to hold up the sky. A woman can now choose her own way to serve, and the needs of the world have never been greater. It is up to each woman to find her own calling. Greatly inspired by women like my mother, I started a movement to encourage women in the United States to step forward in giving to the United Way, which became a billion-dollar initiative. During my years as U.S. Ambassador to Finland, I was engaged in a women's initiative to encourage women across the world to become business entrepreneurs through the Women Business Leaders Summit. I was also privileged to serve on the Habitat for Humanity international board and saw firsthand the incredible role of women in building homes for families in dire need of decent housing. Currently, I am the Chairman of the Board of the American Red Cross. Through these efforts, I see great needs with my own eyes—and I am inspired to continue to do my part in holding up the sky, as the authors of this book are doing.

Among the many hats Linda Fuller wears, one of the most profound is her co-founding of Habitat for Humanity, building homes throughout the world for those in need. By the end of 2005, Habitat will have built some 200,000 homes in countries around the world. Her new Fuller Center for Housing is likely to further impact citizens of the world.

Donna Schuller holds up the sky through her influence in the many roles she lives, including being a minister's wife at Crystal Cathedral, leading Crystal Cathedral Conferences for women, and practicing as a nutritionist for women. Her influence, too, is felt worldwide.

Bettie Youngs has influenced thousands of people in the many hats she wears, from educator to administrator, from university president to Board member. As an author of inspirational and spiritual books, she has reached millions of readers in countries all over the world. But while this is large-scale stuff, as each of these women would tell you, they began it with just one step, and then another, and another. Side-by-side, *woman-to-woman*, they have made a difference.

And so can you. What's important is that we see our influence as important and all-powerful. Bettering the lives of our sisters and their families is one of the many ways women can be a blessing to each other and to the world, as this book reveals. But each of us has our own contribution to make. You may not start a charitable organization, lead a religious conference, or mold young minds in the classroom as these authors have done, but you have your own place in the world—beginning in your own home and your community.

So whatever our paths, all of us gain wisdom and are continuously challenged to grow in our spiritual lives. The uniqueness of this book lies in the personal and Scriptural insights by three outstanding women in hugely influential roles in our times who can help us to do just that. Through the sharing of wisdom, *woman-to-woman*, we each have the potential to hold up our own little part of the sky. This heartfelt and most illuminating book will inspire, challenge, and move you to be the woman that God created you to be.

—Bonnie McElveen-Hunter

The Honorable Bonnie McElveen-Hunter, Chairman, American Red Cross, and CEO, Pace Communications

Introduction

t is with a great deal of reverence and honor that we write this book for our "sisters" everywhere. Our desire in bringing these words to you stems from each of us having worked with women in various roles and capacities for the better part of our professional and personal lives, be it in conducting workshops around the globe to founding various organizations for women, or simply because as mothers, wives, and daughters, we share a similar spirit. Whether we've met at the yearly women's conference sponsored by Crystal Cathedral Ministries, on a Habitat for Humanity build site somewhere in the world, or through one of our books for women—or have never met at all—we are all women of the Earth and children of God. Always our commitment is to better the lives of our sisters—and families—around the world.

Women are very near and dear to our hearts, and in *Woman to Woman Wisdom*, our goal is to share with you some of the many lessons—from "tears to trophies," as women say—we've learned through experiences common to most women. These lessons are important because they confirm what women already know: it's about seeing life's ups and downs with the eyes of our hearts—our willingness to trust that God's loving hands are at work in our lives, giving us meaning and purpose.

Harriet Lerner once remarked, "The rules and roles of our families and society make it especially difficult for women to define ourselves apart from the wishes and expectations of others." There is much truth in this. For most women, the musings of our hearts and the private conversations we hold—often the basis of our prayers—center on how we are feeling and faring in relationship. Perhaps this is what makes women so emotionally literate, our conversations with other women so intensely rich, and our prayers so focused on the well-being of others. Certainly our hearts cry out to God when a loved one falls prey to illness, addiction, or depression, or the man in our life no longer looks at us with loving eyes.

But women also turn to each other. Because women understand the journey a woman's heart pursues, we intuitively know each other. We're familiar with the issues with which a woman's heart concerns itself: Whether a woman's prayers are for the safety of her children or caring for aging parents, or in pining for the days of her own life that have passed all too quickly, women know of the deep soul-searching that goes on within a woman's heart. Whether we are trying to establish bonds or break free of them, we're well acquainted with the hopes and dreams that both burden and give flight to the heart. We're familiar with the emotions of a heart in agony over choosing whether to ascend upward and onward in a career, or whether to downsize goals and needs in order to be there for the people in her life. We know of the joys and the sorrows that make a call upon the heart of a woman, wherever she may live.

Because we know the motivations of a woman's heart, we share other women's concerns as if they were our own. We needn't live in oppression to pray for and support relief for women who do. We need not be a parent to know of the joy in holding a newborn or to understand the strain arising from the monumental responsibility of being a parent. Ours is a common bond, a sisterhood. Instinctually borne within our hearts are the hopes and dreams for the safety of our world and its human family. And so we talk with one another, offering support, comfort, and encouragement. These exchanges offer more than camaraderie: Women discover that whatever our paths, from trophies to tears, encased within the experiences of our lives is a wisdom the soul reveres.

The entries in this book highlight "woman wisdom"—experiences that women know matter at the end of the day, because they teach us what is important and what is not and show us what is real and lasting in life. As we explore these themes together, we hope that you will use the Questions for Discussion provided at the end of each entry to gain further insight into your own thoughts and feelings, as well as a springboard for discussion within your women's group or circle of women friends. We've also included a Scripture for Reflection for each topic, a passage from the Bible that supports learning more about God's Word and His promise to give us love and guidance on the theme being discussed. And, finally, we've included a Prayer for Today, an example to encourage you to have a talk with your Father about a similar concern going on in your life.

So from our hearts to yours, may we say that it is our fervent hope that this book will help you to draw closer to God, trusting that within the experiences of the life laid before you is the opportunity to use your wise and discerning heart to be used by God as He creates miracles within the lives of our sisters everywhere. This is just one more way women can be a blessing to each other and the world.

the authors—Bettie, Linda, and Donna

"Who Am I?" Is Not About Self-Esteem

● ● ● Bettie B. Youngs

Regardless of the roles we're acting out or the circumstance of our lives, we are each, quite simply, a soul in search of our Creator.

Do you sometimes take stock of the many hats you wear and think, *I'm wife, mom, chauffer, head cook, lover, friend, businesswoman—not to mention president of No One Knows What I Do Unless I Don't Do It, Inc.—so, why is it, then, that even with this full house of roles, I still ask, "But who am I?"* Many women think this very thing. And so, off we go on a search to find the "real me." We seek the advice of friends and the gurus of the self-help world, all who send us on wild-goose chases to set boundaries, better manage our time, or build our self-esteem. We buy a new Day-Timer, demand our fair share of daily hugs, and learn the art of saying, "I love me" more. But still we end up wanting. Why? Because the search for self-identity is *not* about self-esteem. It's not about multitasking or the number of hugs we get or however many kisses we manage to blow ourselves in the mirror (without feeling more than a little silly for having done so). Such approaches are not only superficial; they are misguided. Worse, they derail us from the discovery of who we really are.

Who are we? One's true identity is neither a mystery nor elusive.

Finding ourselves is about acknowledging a simple truth: regardless of the roles we're acting out or the circumstances of our lives, we are each, quite simply, a soul in search of our Creator. Shaped in God's image, imbued with a soul that has eternal value, "who we are" is, for each of us, a child of our heavenly Father, an heir to His kingdom.

There is great wisdom in knowing who we are. Nothing could be more important than to ask, *Who am I?* And nothing is more freeing than knowing the answer. Whatever the issue or situation that we find ourselves in—be it momentary inundation in parenting, strained or estranged relationships, concern over lifestyle or earning a living, appeasing the cries of unmet childhood needs, or reclaiming parts of ourselves that were unfairly given or taken away—knowing with certainty *who we are* short-circuits any befuddlement or hesitation as to what direction we must *now* take.

When life showers down roses, or rains only their thorns, either way, the person we see staring back in the mirror is a child belonging to our great heavenly Father. Accepting this birthright means that in spite of the many twists and turns in the roads our lives take, we *know* who we are. We must *know* and *live* who we are. It is an obligation—an honor, but not a burden—to reflect God's love.

During those questioning times—would the real me please raise your hand?—remind yourself *who* you really are. You may be spouse, mother, pal, entrepreneur, chief cook and bottle washer, taxi driver, and more, but the grace, strength, love, and leadership you bring to these roles will look and feel different when you are clear about your true identity.

● ● ● Questions for Discussion:

1. Who are *you*?

2. Do you sometimes feel overwhelmed by the roles you occupy?

3. If so, what brings you to that point?

4. In what ways is the Bible the best self-help book ever written?

5. How does a woman best discover her true identity as God's heir?

● ● ● Scripture for Reflection: *God has made you also [His] heir.* —Galatians 4:7

● ● ● Prayer for Today: *Dear God, as busy as I am and as one day most assuredly melts into the next, I sometimes ask myself if there is more to life than the many hats I wear. I know that I am needed, wanted, and loved. Still, on some days, God, it feels like something is missing in my life. I do know that You are my God and that I am Your child—an heir. Your heir. On those days when the world drowns out my knowing who I am, please remind me, heart to heart, that, apart from all the ways I serve others, serving You first gives rise to my true identity—an awesome identity. Thank You for this enormous gift and for the price paid for it through Your beloved Son.*

2

If I Had My Life to Live Over . . .

● ● ● Linda C. Fuller

Every day on Earth is a gift from God—another chance to live life to the fullest.

One of my favorite personalities was Erma Bombeck. When she was alive, I read her newspaper columns and books every chance I got. Once I was privileged to hear her speak at a women's conference sponsored by Rosalynn Carter and several other former First Ladies. She was so funny and full of wisdom. Unfortunately, we lost this amazing woman to cancer, but her writings continue to influence people.

One of the pieces she wrote after she found out she was dying from cancer was "If I Had My Life to Live Over." Have you ever thought about what you'd do differently if you got another chance to start your life over? For example, when you think about how you've lived your life to date, do you have regrets about things that you did—or didn't do? Do you have dreams you failed to pursue or wishes you pushed aside? Did you make promises you didn't keep or put things off that never got done? Here are some of the things that Erma wished she had done during her lifetime:

● I would have gone to bed when I was sick instead of pretending the Earth would go into a holding pattern if I weren't there for the day.

● I would have burned the pink candle sculpted like a rose before it melted in storage.

● I would have taken the time to listen to my grandfather ramble about his youth.

● Instead of wishing away nine months of pregnancy, I'd have cherished every moment and realized that the wonderment growing inside me was the only chance in life to assist God in a miracle.

It shouldn't take a cancer diagnosis to prompt us to think about our own lives so far and what we'd do differently. Have you made your own "If I Had My Life to Live Over" list? I have. Some of the things on my list include:

● I would have insisted that my husband and our older children take more responsibility for caring for the younger ones in our family.

● I would have made more time for my own needs rather than being consumed with fulfilling others'.

● I would have found a good decorator sooner before wasting so much money on unwise choices of colors and furniture.

● I would have spent more time reading the Bible and praying before jumping headlong into a busy day.

● I would have learned sooner to stop watering my plants when they looked sick, because overwatering was their problem!

● I would have made a greater effort to feed my family more hugs rather than elaborate, time-consuming new dishes.

● I would have developed friendships with women sooner rather than waiting until my fifties when my menopausal symptoms prompted me to seek them out (and what life-savers they were!).

Of course, it's impossible to live life over, but we can make the best of the time that is left. Learn from your regrets—it's never too late to start anew. No, you can't live your life over again, but you can learn from your successes and failures as you move forward. It's important to start now on your own list of things you'd do if you could live your life over.

Ecclesiastes 8:7–8 tells us, "Since no man [or woman] knows the future, who can tell him what is to come? No man has power over the wind to contain it; so no one has power over the day of his death." This means we have no idea how much time we have left—it could be an hour or fifty years. Therefore, we shouldn't waste any time in recalling what we missed out on—and then pursuing those things today. As we're told in Haggai 1:5, "Give careful thought to your ways." Make every moment count. Live every day as if it were your last. Every day on earth is a gift—another chance to live life to the fullest.

● ● ● Questions for Discussion:

1. Are there certain things you wish you had done as a child? A teenager? A younger woman?

2. Is it too late, or could you still fulfill at least some of those wishes?

3. Are regrets always bad, or can they teach us something?

4. Why do you think God is pleased when we give careful thought to how we spend our days?

● ● ● **Scripture for Reflection:** *Turn us back to You, O Lord, and we will be restored; renew our days as of old.* —Lamentations 5:21

● ● ● **Prayer for Today:** *My heavenly Friend, thank You for the gift of every day that I have on earth. As I think back on my life, there are so many things that I did wrong . . . or failed to do . . . or never found time for. Please give me the wisdom to pursue those things I've put off and to make amends for my mistakes. Guide me toward a more meaningful life so that when I come to the end of my journey, I will have no regrets.*

3

You Can Start Over

● ● ● Donna Schuller

That our lives feel in shambles can be exactly the motivation
we need to realign our priorities, and to get right with life.

People frequently ask me how I met my husband, Robert
Schuller. I don't mind repeating the story, because it is
the perfect example of God's hand in helping us to start
over when we've hit a dead end. No matter how hopeless or
dark our lives become, God has a plan to bring us back into the
light. This is what happened to both Robert and me when our
paths crossed.

At that time in my life, starting over wasn't an option—it was
a necessity. The airline I'd been working for filed for bankruptcy,
so I lost my job after seven years of employment. On top of that,
my husband of only a few years decided he no longer wanted to
be married! I subsequently moved back to my hometown of
Laguna Beach, California. It was a low point for me, a time when
I felt as if all my hopes and dreams had been stripped from me. I
was alone. I had all but disconnected from God.

Little did I realize that while I'd placed God fairly low on my
list of priorities, I was at the top of His. While to me my life looked
a hopeless mess, to God my life looked perfect—perfectly ready to

receive His plan for me. While I may have been oblivious to God, He had His sights on me: God had been there all along, right by my side, preparing me for what was to come—His plan for me. And though I didn't know it at the time, Robert Schuller was to be a part of His plan for me. And me for Robert!

I first saw Robert Schuller in the parking garage of our apartment building. He was carrying a very large briefcase, and since there were few young people living in my building, I assumed he was a door-to-door salesman. I would learn later that he was indeed a kind of salesman, all right! He was a minister, so he sold hope, faith, and God's love—things I certainly needed at this low point in my life.

Months went by before I saw him again, but one day looking out my window, I spied him on the balcony below. Something about him intrigued me, and I really wanted to meet him, so I hurriedly brushed my hair and freshened up, but by the time I had finished, he was already gone.

I decided to go down to the beach to take a walk along the shore. Ten minutes later, I saw a man walking toward me, and it was him. There was no one else on the beach. I still remember what he was wearing: blue jeans, a red plaid shirt, a beige Windbreaker, and brown cowboy boots. There he was, tall, dark, and, I might add, very handsome!

We said hello and began to talk as we walked along together. He told me his name and that he was a minister. (I would learn later from my roommate that he ministered at Crystal Cathedral—which she knew because she and her family watched *The Hour of Power*, an internationally televised church service.) As we walked, he told me that his wife had asked for a divorce and that they had two little children, then ages two and five. In the first minutes of our walk, I was happily thinking, *I've met someone!* But when he told me about all that was going on for him—including two small children, I remember thinking, *Oh, gosh, I'm just getting out of a difficult situation—and this guy sounds complicated too!* And of course, there was the fact that he was a minister—that was a bit intimidating as well. I hadn't been to church in several years.

But he was starting over too, and that greatly appealed to me. We began seeing each other, as I knew we would. Right from the beginning, there was a mutual respect and admiration for each other. As our relationship deepened, I knew this was more than a chance meeting. Somehow I just knew that God had brought us together. Time went by, and we enjoyed being together. And we were equally happy to be helping each other through what was a very difficult time in both our lives. By early summer we had fallen in love, and nearly a year after that first conversation, we were married.

Talk about a new beginning! Still, I can't say it was all a honeymoon from there on out. As destined and blessed as our meeting was, this was not your typical "boy meets girl, and they live happily ever after" sort of life. Being in Robert's life was a huge adjustment: he was a minister with many responsibilities. The church sees a minister's wife as a role defined within certain dimensions of the church, so being his wife meant I would have church responsibilities as well. And Robert was the father of two small children; hence, I became an instant mom. At that point I'd not been a mother; what did I know about parenting small children?

But these two roles—being a minister's wife and a stepmom to two young children—were waiting for me, ready or not. I had myself to deal with, as well. In some ways, I was still coming to terms with the broken parts of my own past. Clearly, I needed to know myself and become a confident person in my own right before I was really ready to take on the leadership roles into which I'd been thrust. Love had delivered me a new life. It was a huge job with enormous responsibilities, and—prepared or not—I had signed up for it! But God never gives us more than we can handle, and He has been faithful to Robert and me. Just recently we celebrated twenty years of marriage!

Have you ever had to start over? How did you feel about that? It can be scary, can't it? Still, that our lives feel in shambles can be exactly the motivation we need to realign our priorities and to get right with life. Reaching a dead end is as good a time as any to start over! What we discover in the process is that starting over is an opportunity from God to rethink things. Have you ever looked at dead ends in that light? It's a really helpful perspective.

So where do you start? If you are at a point in your life when all seems a bit overwhelming—if you feel unsure and unclear what to do, where to go, and why—have a talk with God. Ask Him what His plan is for you. When your life seems the most chaotic, it may be because God wants you to take a look at—and reorder—your priorities. When we're at a loss, God will help us succeed: "Commit to the LORD whatever you do, and your plans will succeed," we learn in Proverbs 16:3.

If you are "unequally yoked" (2 Corinthians 6:14 KJV) to your job or your partner or you feel out of sync or disconnected in your life, if you need to start over, hold on to hope. God takes the brokenness in our lives, and through His love He forgives and He heals. He builds us—if we but let Him into our hearts. Have the faith and humility to let Him in. In this way, you can and will experience God's love—and then you will begin living His divine plan for your life. There is one, and sometimes starting over is the only way to get to it. Trust that no matter how hopeless or dark your life becomes, God has a plan to bring you back into the light. Just as He did for me.

● ● ● Questions for Discussion:

1. Have there been times in your life when you needed to start over?

2. Did the thought of starting over scare you or fill you with excitement?

3. How did God re-create you as a result of this challenging time?

4. Did you have a close relationship with God at this time, or were you estranged from God?

5. Is God's plan working in your life, or is that yet to come?

● ● ● Scripture for Reflection: *Therefore, if anyone is in Christ, he is a new creation; the old has gone, the new has come!* —2 Corinthians 5:17

● ● ● Prayer for Today: *Dear God, during those times in life when it's necessary to start over, help me not to be filled with fear, but to trust in You. It is at these lowest and most insecure times that You really prove Your love for us—thank You for that. Help us to reach out to You, and remind us that, with faith, there will be a brighter tomorrow! Thank You for being there for us, Lord.*

Mothers Are Sisters to Each Other

● ● ● Bettie B. Youngs

*Let us sisters everywhere join together in prayer asking God
to hear our collective pleas for those whose lives are in jeopardy because our humanity has not yet fully grasped God's
command that we love each other as He so loves us.*

When my daughter was an infant, I looked forward to
the time when she would be able to explore the
world—without being a danger to herself. In grade
school, like all kids her age, her boundless energy and immediate trust of seemingly everything and everyone required constant
explanations and reminders of rules for being and staying safe.
Junior high ushered in an endless love of sports and, with it, a
fearless, competitive spirit. So, willing or not, I had to get over
my skittishness in watching doctors sew up my little kid.

Next came a tireless exploration of the many options available to a pack of precocious preteens, so boundaries and curfews
had to be put in place—and I had to learn the art of using effective (versus *ineffective*) tones when saying, "No." Suddenly, hor-
mones were raging, bringing an onslaught of do-or-die moods
and an ever-changing list of girlfriends and boyfriends, and I
became a clinical psychologist, with my drama-queen teen as my
full-time caseload.

Then came the day when her beloved pony was traded for a

different kind of horsepower, and now being out and about with her new wheels and with many friends occupied a good portion of her waking hours—and became a source of sleep deprivation for me. Abruptly she has become a young adult, trying out her wings to see how high and far she can soar. And just as I worried when she was little that she might stick her finger in a light socket or be treated badly by another child, I still worry about her—whether she is attending an oversold rock concert with newfound friends or embarking on a mission abroad at a time of heightened terrorist activity.

Always, always, my child's safety is on my mind.

For me, this sense of obligation began with my pregnancy, but the moment my daughter was born, the fragility of life was made ever so real, so protecting her became a compelling duty. I knew her life was mine to protect and that I would commit to it at all costs. Such feelings paved the way for my realizing that this new "lens on the world" is true for every parent, and I now know and care deeply about parents everywhere. Whereas once I sympathized with parents of sick, injured, or missing children, parenthood meant that I now feel *with* them. When I watch the evening news and hear about the casualties of hatred at work in our world, I know that everywhere out there are mothers like me who hope and pray for their children's safety.

Mothers share a common bond, a sisterhood of sorts. Because the hopes and dreams we each hold for the safety of our children are seeds instinctually borne within our hearts, may we unite in a common quest for peace and prosperity for all children—His children. Let us sisters everywhere join together in prayer asking God to hear our collective pleas for those parents and children whose lives are in jeopardy because our humanity has not yet fully grasped God's command that we love each other as He so loves us. All women are sisters; let our kinship be a blessing to parents everywhere.

● ● ● Questions for Discussion:

1. Are you a "sister" to women all over the world?

2. In what ways can women unite to make the world a safer place for all children?

3. Do you pray for other parents and children, even those you have never met?

4. What one thing can you do today for your "sisters" that will be pleasing to your Father?

● ● ● Scripture for Reflection: *From heaven the LORD looks down and sees all mankind; from his dwelling place he watches all who live on earth—he who forms the hearts of all, who considers everything they do.* —Psalm 33:13–15

● ● ● Prayer for Today: *Oh, Father, thank You for my precious child and for the possession of a heart that fervently seeks to protect her. Having known the joys and fears of protecting the life You sent to me to guard and guide, I pray for all mothers and fathers in the world and for their children's safety. Help us to all desire to be soldiers in spreading Your Word. Grant that we will all come to know You so that we might call a truce to the hatred that gives way to the persecution of Your children. We pray, Father, that You hear our collective prayers for parents the world over whose own children are suffering due to our failure to love each other as You so commanded us to do. Unite us, Father, and remind us that we are all Your children. And that we must each love, care about, and look out for each other.*

5

The Secret to Staying in Love

● ● ● Linda C. Fuller

*Staying in love and staying with someone
are very different goals, aren't they?*

Can you remember when you first fell in love? I can! I was
seventeen, and my boyfriend was twenty-three. He said
that it was "love at first sight" for him. I liked him, but I
can't say that I was thinking about "forever." I simply wanted to go
out with a tall guy so I could wear high heels!

After we'd dated for a few months, this young man, Millard
Fuller, told me how much he loved me and that he had plans for
us to marry. That's right. He never proposed, but rather, he *told* me
we would get married. At that time, I didn't object because by
then I loved him too, and I thought he was a neat guy as well as a
"good catch." My parents, however, weren't too keen on my mar-
rying a man six years older than myself. But they liked that he was
already showing signs of being a talented entrepreneur, was nearly
finished with law school, and had aspirations to make something
of himself.

Now we've been together forty-five years and are proud to say
that we have four outstanding adult offspring and eight amazing
grandkids.

Forty-five years! That's a long time. Have you ever wondered how some people stay married for life? Of course, the more valuable question might be, how can couples stay in love *forever*? Staying *in* love and staying *with* a spouse are very different, aren't they? Certainly, doing either takes time, effort, and many prayers. It wasn't always easy, but I think my husband and I have finally discovered the secret to staying in love—a goal we've both worked at very hard now for a long time.

Like a lot of couples, we've had great times, good times, and those times when we felt like two adults merely living under the same roof. There were tough times, fun times, and times when we came close to losing our marriage. In fact, in our sixth year of marriage, we briefly separated. We think back on that now and shudder to imagine that we came so close to losing each other! The good news is that, for all that had broken us apart, we still loved each other, and we knew that our marriage was worth fighting for. Today we have our family and what we think of as "God's 'bigger' plan for our lives"—the creation and ongoing outreach ministry of building affordable housing through Habitat for Humanity and the Fuller Center for Housing—to show for it.

So what is the secret to a love relationship that lasts forever? First, each person must be committed to the relationship and willing to give 100 percent (as opposed to thinking in terms of fifty-fifty, or worse, less than that). And it's doing those things that keep the love, play, and passion alive—making time for each other, shared experiences, fun getaways that allow a reprieve from the daily routines of life, things like this. But the real secret to a great marriage is to give God a place—His place—in the relationship. In a truly happy marriage, God is the glue that keeps love, honor, respect, and a willingness to hang in there "in sickness and in health" possible.

Perhaps you, like Millard and me, said your wedding vows in front of family and friends—and in the presence of God. We asked God to bless us—*and our marriage*. We sometimes forget this, don't we, the keeping of God at the very center of our lives and asking for His continued blessings upon the marriage? In the early years of our marriage, Millard and I did a pretty good job of this. Both of us had come from families who regularly attended church, so right from the beginning, we had all the intentions in the world of staying God-centered. As a young couple, we even started a church in our home, one that eventually occupied a small building.

But as time went on, we slowly allowed our attention to shift away from our spiritual lives, spending more and more time and attention on our outer lives. Millard, for example, spent increasingly more hours on his rapidly expanding business. I was caring for our small children and earning my college degree. We seemed to have little or no time for spiritual nourishment other than attending church on Sundays.

The result was disastrous: the price we paid for all of our success and achievement almost cost us our marriage. That our marriage was on the rocks brought us to our knees, literally. What we discovered was that, though we had all but abandoned God, He had not abandoned us. Through prayer, God let us know that He had called us together and that He *still* had plans for our lives. In other words, He wasn't done with us yet! He called us to give our lives totally to Him and His continued purpose. We said yes, and it's made all the difference. Because of that awesome call and commitment, joy filled our hearts and healed our broken relationship. Since that time, with each passing year our love for each other has only grown stronger. Today, our lives are richer and more meaningful than ever.

We learned a valuable lesson: love, no matter how strong, doesn't maintain itself without being nourished. But love is also most durable when it is governed and protected by the Father of love, our heavenly Father. As my husband and I can attest, "forever" is possible if you first stay in love with God.

God's love for us is remarkable. And God wants our love for each other to be remarkable too. Why should we settle for less?

We don't have to. If your marriage is all but lifeless, if you're feeling unloved and disconnected from your mate, if your marriage is broken, a good counselor can help, but only God can mend it. If you're looking for a place to start, begin with God's advice: "Be kind and compassionate to one another, forgiving each other, just as in Christ God forgave you" (Ephesians 4:32). God's love for us is the glue that will keep us strong and hold us together—if we but issue the invitation for Him to enter into our lives.

● ● ● Questions for Discussion:

1. Do you remember how you felt the first time you fell in love?

2. Did that same feeling last forever, or did real life intrude?

3. What qualities are important for a lasting marriage?

4. What is the ultimate glue that will keep a relationship together?

5. Have you fallen in love with God? In what way does this serve your relationships?

● ● ● Scripture for Reflection: *And now these three remain: faith, hope and love. But the greatest of these is love.* —1 Corinthians 13:13

● ● ● Prayer for Today: *Dear God, please help my husband and me to realize that we need to make You the center of our relationship. We are so blessed by the incredible love that You have for us. Show us how to maintain that same amazing love with each other. Teach us to be kind and patient with each other; to make time for each other; to treat each other respectfully. But most of all, teach us to fall in love with You, with all our hearts, so that this love will be a lasting influence on our lives together.*

6

Parent Me, Heavenly Father

● ● ● Donna Schuller

*For all that has been part and parcel for my life, I've become
a stronger and more confident and capable woman.*

Scripture tells us that God doesn't give us more than we
can handle. Have you ever doubted it? I certainly have!
There have been oh so many times when I've found
myself in a situation and said, "No way, God; give me a break here!
I'm not ready for this!" It was just such an occasion on my twenty-
ninth birthday, when I got some stunning news: Robert had been
awarded full custody of his two small children, ages three and six!

I was still a newlywed, married only two and a half months.
Never in my wildest imagination did I think this would be a part
of my first weeks of marriage—but it was so. The children would
stay with us during the week and visit their mother only on the
weekends. I hardly considered myself ready to parent small children. Up to that point, I had no children of my own. I had been
a flight attendant, model, and traveling sales representative—but
none of these roles had prepared me for raising kids. And since
my dad had died in a car accident when I was thirteen, in many
ways I still thought I could use some parenting myself. How could
I ever handle the day-to-day care of two little kids?

The children arrived, bringing with them only a small, wicker, picnic-type basket filled with neatly folded clothes, enough to last just through the week. You can only imagine what was going through their little heads: Angie was timid and looked sad. Bobby was bouncy and playful. Just imagine what was going through *my* head! I felt sad to see them separated from their mother—and wondered how she and these little children were feeling about that. And of course, as difficult as this was for the mom and children, I was wondering just how long this new arrangement would last—the courts had granted full-time custody; did they mean for now, or was it going to be permanent? But there they stood, two little children. I remember thinking, *Good-bye newlywed; hello stepmother!*

I had been right in the assessment that life as I knew it (and had anticipated it) was over. From the next day forward, it was full-on parenting for me! There was a challenge at every corner! The first day I showed up at school to get Angie, who was in first grade, the teacher shoved a pile of books at me and in a very firm and official way said, "She is so far behind that you will have to work hard for several weeks for her to catch up." I remember feeling so helpless and overwhelmed, thinking, *How? I'm not equipped to do this!*

This was the beginning of what would prove to be one of many tough lessons I would learn. I had to learn how to help Angie with her homework and how to groom her long, pretty hair. I had to learn that little Bobby would cry if I cut his peanut butter and jelly sandwich the wrong way and that he was afraid of the dark, so either Robert or myself would have to stay on his bedroom floor until he fell asleep at night. I also had to learn how to draw them a bath—with bubbles—and how to read stories, cook the food they liked, comfort them when they fell down and got hurt, and clean up vomit in the middle of the night. And when they were crabby or misbehaved, like all normal children, I remember telling my husband that when we had kids of our own, they would never act that way. (I would eat my words on that one; Robert and I eventually had two children together.)

There were times early on when I felt so besieged with obligations that I contemplated leaving. But rarely did I end up any further than seated in my car in the garage. I'd sit there and just bawl my eyes out until the frustration had subsided—at least a little. Then I'd go back inside—feeling absolutely terrible, guilty, and embarrassed after one of these bouts. Why couldn't I figure this parenting thing out? Why was it so difficult? Two little children and it felt like I needed a PhD in child psychology—as well as a yearlong vacation (without the kids, of course!).

Eventually I learned that what I really needed most was to change my expectations. I now see that part of the difficulty in blending a family has to do with unrealistic expectations. I think we each have an idea about how things are going to work, when, in fact, we haven't a clue. Often things play out in ways we can never predict. Each day brings to the table its very own set of dramas. When things don't go as planned, we're disappointed. And annoyed. This goes for everyone.

Robert had his expectations. He expected me to take care of the kids while he did his job. Among my many expectations were that the kids be perfect little angels—beginning with their respecting me. I expected them to keep their rooms clean and neat, their toys picked up, and, well, I won't bore you with the list. It was a very long one! And, of course, the kids had expectations of their own—often conflicting ones, I learned. For example, they expected me to act and treat them the same way their mother did—until they wanted some special favor—and then they expected to "work" me and not have me react as their mother did. Oh, yes, expectations are at the heart of the push and pull in families—especially blended families.

It wasn't just my expectations of mothering that had to be readjusted. So did the expectations I had with my new husband. For one, I expected him to understand what sacrifices I was making by being a stepmother and to shoulder a great deal of the parenting load. But he was busy building a church and keeping food on the table—and so the role was mostly mine.

We had alone time only on the weekends, so perhaps I even felt cheated out of being a more carefree bride, especially in the early days of my marriage. I wanted more time with my husband. And I felt cheated out of easygoing times. Because my husband and I were the weekday parents, we were the ones with more rules and, in the children's eyes, less fun. I resented that we had strict bedtimes and homework, while the kids' mom got to go to Disneyland and the movies with them on the weekends.

Many years have passed. Robert and I had children of our own, which was an entirely new set of demands—and, to say the least, a training ground of its own! I'm happy to say I've hung in there, and, oh, what a rich experience it has been. In having my own children, and in helping to raise Robert's children—whom I truly love as my own—I can honestly say with all that has been part and parcel for my life, I've become a stronger and more confident and capable woman. God has been good to me and has blessed me in a million ways. For one, He has forgiven me for all my inexperience and mistakes. He stood by my side in those early days of my marriage when I didn't think I could do it. He continues to love me through life's ups and downs today. And when I look at the two fine adults that Angie and Bobby (now called Robby) have become, I know the privilege it is to have been a part of two young human beings' lives in a time when they needed extra love and guidance.

I can see that with His power and unfailing love, God was there for me, guiding me and teaching me—and parenting me when I needed it the most. By loving these children, God was loving me and helping me to heal the wounds of my childhood. Through these children, God was a parent to me when I needed loving as well as healing from my own unfinished business of childhood angst.

Have you ever had times when you didn't know how to handle things—times when you just wanted to get in your car and drive away from it all? We all do. But there is a better alternative: when you're feeling overwhelmed, ask God to help you lean on Him, as David did in Psalm 94:18: "When I said, 'My foot is slipping,' your love, O LORD, supported me." Let Him be not only your Father, but the parent you need in times when nothing short of a parent will do. God is the greatest parent of all. Trust that it is so.

● ● ● Questions for Discussion:

1. In what ways has God not given you more than you can handle?

2. Do you ever feel overwhelmed by the stresses of raising your children or stepchildren?

3. If you're raising a blended family, what unique challenges do you face?

4. What can we learn from God about being a good parent?

5. Was there a time in life when you felt that God was parenting you?

● ● ● Scripture for Reflection: *Be still, and know that I am God.* —Psalm 46:10

● ● ● Prayer for Today: *Dear Father, You gave birth to all the children of the world by breathing life into each one of us. As we continue to grow and mature in You, help us to be strong disciples for our youth and to realize that You never give us more than we can handle. When the demands of parenting overwhelm us, help us to be as patient and loving with our children as You are with us. Parent us so that we might be better role models to those who need our guidance and love.*

7

Setting Suns

● ● ● Bettie B. Youngs

Nothing could have been more loving a gift than the eye-opening experience of watching my mother close down her life—for in it was great insight as to how we must live.

M y mother lived every day of her life basking joyously in the sunlight of God's love. She simply loved and served her Lord. We children loved her all the more for this example: what a blessing it was to know that when God called her home, He would welcome my mother into His kingdom with out-stretched arms. Never was this knowledge more comforting than when my mother learned the final days of life were upon her. While the reality that, in the not-too-distant future, our mother would not be there to talk to, and to hug was painful, nothing could have been more loving a gift than the eye-opening experi-ence of watching her close down her life—for in it was great insight as to how we children must live our own lives from this day forward.

From the time her cancer was diagnosed, our mother was given three months to live. Accepting this sentence as "yet another phase of my life," as she called it, she went about, in her words, "completing" things. She began by visiting each of her children, and then friends, relatives, and community members, telling them

29

how much she'd appreciated and loved knowing them, as well as asking for forgiveness if she had wronged them in any way.

Next Mom went through closets, cabinets, and drawers, boxing and distributing certain mementos and photo albums to her children and grandchildren—things she wanted each of us to have. After that she gathered us children around to help her, as she referred to it, "tie up loose ends." She assigned each of us things to do, such as helping her select a casket, writing her obituary, locating her favorite hymns and Scripture to be used in the funeral service pamphlet, preparing a mailing list that would be used to send out notices to friends and relatives who lived far away, and so on. It was quite an experience—heart wrenching, but logical, practical, generous, thoughtful, and loving.

Then came the photo phase—a ritual in which Mom went around the house looking at the many photos of her family over the years, one more time. She would pick up a picture, study it, dust it, and either return it to its place or turn it upside down. Seeing her do this, I asked her what it meant. "Oh," she said, referring to the picture she held in her hands of my sister and me as small girls in cute, look-alike sundresses, snuggling in our parents' laps, "I just love you all so much. I love your father, and I love each of my children and their children. Look, this was taken in Seattle . . ." and then she proceeded to tell me about this treasured time in her life as a young married woman with small children. With the telling of the memory came tears, and then a decision: she returned it—upright—on the shelf. "I think maybe I'm not so done with this memory," she said.

Taking her in my arms, I asked, "Mom, what is this experience like, the closing down of one's life?"

"Well," she replied, "going home to God is tearful, but not fearful. I'm not afraid. I am ready to be with my heavenly Father. Preparing to go home is what this lifetime is about, so there is a joyful love in that this is what I'm doing now. It's a feeling unlike any love I've experienced, actually—including the love a mother feels for her children or a wife feels for her husband. So it's my obligation now to let go of everything that was a part of this life. Some things are easy. Others are not so easy. But whenever I feel heavyhearted, I also feel God's hand upon my shoulder, comforting me, and all I can do is say, 'Thank You, Father, for the children You gave me, and all the things I've experienced in this world.' At these times, my love for my Lord is so immense that I'm literally drawn to my heavenly home."

And then my mother lovingly counseled, "We will be together again. Please try not to get too caught up in the way the world would want to make you believe is important. In the end, all that really matters is that we've found our way home to our Creator."

One week later, everything in my mother's house had been dusted and turned over. And on that day my mother allowed her illness to take her to bed and shortly thereafter, to carry her beyond the sunset and into the light of a life she confidently knew offered more love than this world ever could.

As poignant as all this was, in her closing minutes of life, my mother offered up a wisdom that all of God's children most assuredly know: *God is for real.* She assured her family of the presence of God upon her, that He was reaching for her hand. The peace on her face and the sweetness of her parting smile affirmed that our mother was indeed now walking with her heavenly Father. I feel so blessed that someone I trust as loving me more than anyone else on this earth had affirmed that God is the God He promised to be.

Only God knows for sure when we'll enjoy our last sunset here on earth. I guess my mother was fortunate, because she was given the time to get her affairs in order; to make amends to anyone she may have slighted; to say good-bye to those near and dear; to cherish treasured memories one last time, and then to detach completely from all earthly things. But even if my mother hadn't been given this opportunity it wouldn't have mattered, because she lived every day of her life right with God.

Are your affairs in order? If within months—or minutes—you found yourself face-to-face with God, would you be welcomed with outstretched arms? We often hear the phrase "Live each day as if it were your last." May we do that, so that when it is our time to take that last breath on earth, we, too, will go with the sunshine on our faces, knowing we are firmly in the grasp of God's hands.

● ● ● Questions for Discussion:

1. Are you afraid of dying?

2. Are you right with God?

3. In what ways is being right with God reassuring to your loved ones?

4. In what ways do you have your affairs in order?

5. If you learned God was calling you home, with whom would you need to get right before you could face God with the assurance that He would be pleased with the way you lived among His children?

● ● ● Scripture for Reflection: *Live self-controlled, upright and godly lives in this present age, while we wait for the blessed hope—the glorious appearing of our great God and Savior, Jesus Christ.* —Titus 2:12–13

● ● ● Prayer for Today: *God, one of Your great mysteries is that we don't know how many days we will be granted on earth. We trust You with this great and wondrous mystery. Help us to live every single day in ways that are pleasing to You so that at the end of our days, we can come home to You. Teach us always to walk in the sunshine of Your love. By our words and deeds, help us to prepare for the day when we will walk into Your arms.*

8

The Chipped Ring

● ● ● Linda C. Fuller

Wisdom is listening to the clues that your conscience gives—
so God won't have to hit you in the head with a brick (of His
choice)!

I once heard a story about a man who was planning to rob a store. He picked up a concrete block and threw it as hard as he could at the store window. But the window was made of Plexiglas, and the concrete block bounced back and hit the thief in the head! It knocked him cold, allowing plenty of time for the police to arrive and take him away. This is an amusing account, of course, but it's tragic too. I'd like to think that God was teaching the thief a thing or two about right and wrong.

I remember a time when He taught me a similar lesson. My mother bought a ring for me at a five-and-dime. I was nine years old at the time. The ring had a clear-blue imitation stone in it, and I really liked it. I wore it constantly.

But after a while the blue stone chipped. This really bothered me, every single time I looked at it. So one day I went to the store to see if they had another one. Sure enough, they did. Standing there, an idea popped into my head—one that made my heart pound (which should have been a clue to me right there that God was trying to tell me something). Why not just take the chipped ring off my finger and exchange it for the new one on the table? I knew in my heart that this idea was wrong. Even so, I yielded to temptation.

I exchanged the rings and hurried out of the store.

I didn't say anything for a while, but finally, guilt troubled me so much that I told my mother what I had done. She was shocked but also grateful that I had 'fessed up. She then took me—and my "new" ring—back to the store. We went to the ring section where my old chipped ring was still on display. Apparently, none of the clerks had noticed it. Mother picked up the box containing the chipped ring and had me replace it with the one on my finger.

We then went to the checkout counter with the undamaged ring. I was holding my breath, afraid she'd tell the cashier what I had done, but she paid for it without a word. After leaving the store, Mother took the new ring out of the bag and said simply, "Linda, don't ever do anything like that again." Enough said. She never had to remind me.

Robbery comes in all forms, of course—be it thieving from a store, cheating on a spouse, not instilling right from wrong in our kids, hitting a car in the parking lot and not reporting it, failing to notify the salesclerk that she undercharged us, neglecting our health, and so on. Fortunately for us, "In him we have redemption . . . the forgiveness of sins, in accordance with the riches of God's grace" (Ephesians 1:7). We can come to God, ask for His forgiveness, and accept His marvelous, unmerited favor. But the Bible tells us we must take it one step further: "He who has been stealing must steal no longer, but must work, doing something useful with his own hands, that he may have something to share with those in need" (Ephesians 4:28). We must atone for our mistakes by making things right.

If you've hurt someone, apologize—and mean it. Show repentance by doing good for others. Make something positive come out of a negative situation. Of course, you can listen to all the clues that God gives you through your conscience so as to be an honest person in the first place. That way, God won't have to hit you in the head with a brick (of His choice)!

● ● ● Questions for Discussion:

1. In what way have you taken, and in what way did your conscience convict you?

2. How can you atone for your wrongdoings?

3. Have you experienced the blessing of confessing your wrongdoing and asking for forgiveness?

4. How does God get your attention when you do something wrong?

● ● ● Scripture for Reflection: *You shall not steal.* —Exodus 20:15

● ● ● Prayer for Today: *Dear God, sometimes I am weak and give in to temptations. Please help me to be stronger, that I might resist temptation when it comes knocking. When I fail and commit a wrong, show me how to make it right and earn Your forgiveness. Thank You for giving us the gift of Your Son, that all of our sins might be forgiven.*

9

Comfort in Times of Trouble

● ● ● Donna Schuller

Times of crisis teach us how much we are willing to believe in God, and the degree to which we are willing to trust in Him.

'll never forget the terrifying experience of watching our seventeen-month-old daughter, Christina, topple from a wooden swing set and land on the platform below. It all happened so quickly, right in front of our eyes. Just seconds before, she and her older siblings had been enjoying their playtime together. I immediately picked her up, soothed and comforted her, and checked to see if she'd been injured. It didn't take long for her to recover and wiggle her way out from my hug to resume her running and climbing. Judging by the way she recuperated so quickly, she seemed to be just fine. At the end of the day, she ate dinner and went to bed as usual. Nothing indicated that she was feeling the effects of her spill on the playground.

Everything changed the following morning. While giving her a bath, I discovered a soft, egg-shaped lump on the left side of her tiny skull. Most bruises I had seen before were hard to the touch, but this one was not. We called our pediatrician and explained about Christina's accident the previous day. He advised us to bring her to his office for an examination. After checking her, he sent us to the hospital for an X-ray. The test revealed that our daughter had a depression skull fracture and that the soft swelling was due to synovial fluid leaking out of her skull! Because I was eight months pregnant with our son, I couldn't risk being exposed to radiation, so my husband, Robert, attended to Christina as they prepared to do a CAT scan. Minutes later, her little body disappeared into the donut-shaped machine that would tell us more about the injury she had sustained.

Any parent knows that keeping a seventeen-month-old quiet and completely still for any length of time is nearly impossible, but my husband managed to do it. Our daughter knew that prayer time was a time for quiet, so as she lay on her back with her bottle in her mouth, her little hands clasped around it, her daddy led her in prayer. "Dear God, thank You for Mommy and Daddy and Angie and Bobby and Christina and Grandma and Grandpa," they repeated over and over for the whole five minutes. Miraculously, she didn't move a muscle.

Thank goodness, because the CAT scan revealed that her situation was more dire than we had thought. We met with a neurosurgeon, who told us that our tiny daughter needed emergency brain surgery! The skull needed to be repaired, he told us, and our daughter would probably suffer seizures over the next several years. Surgery was scheduled for the following Monday.

You can only imagine our fear and concern for our little child. We prayed nonstop for our daughter. We also asked God to grant us the clarity to know what to do and for the strength to sustain us so we could do it. We also asked family members, close friends, and the church to begin a prayer chain. God granted all our prayers instantly. Robert's parents urged us to take our daughter for a second opinion. We were seen that afternoon. Upon examination, the head of a neurosurgery department concluded that our daughter's injury was not life-threatening. In fact, we were told that these types of depression skull fractures are quite common in toddlers and that because the skull is still relatively soft, the depression would probably pop back out on its own. He recommended that she *not* have the surgery! Needless to say, we felt as though a tremendous burden had been lifted from our shoulders, and we left in peace. We continued to pray for Christina, and sure enough, within a week she was perfectly normal.

Experiences like these reveal such truth, don't they? In these times we learn there is much truth in the saying "There are no atheists in foxholes." Crisis times teach us how much we are willing to believe in God, and the degree to which we are willing to trust in Him. At times like these, we want to believe that God is present and that He's watching and listening—and protecting. And we readily learn how willing we are to feel the hand of God's love for us and on us. We certainly did. Just as we comforted our daughter after her fall, God was right there with us, comforting us and helping us through this very scary time.

And we learned to hear God directing us. My husband and I asked God to please clarify what we should do. We felt so helpless. God granted us that clarity. Crises are baffling, and yet it was God's hand steering us through our ordeal, giving us the right people at the right time and with the right know-how: God came through. And God got us through. I could feel Him lifting my fear and reassuring me. Yes, we should and must turn to our families and friends in times like these. Certainly, they help support and hold us up. But we must also remember to first turn to our heavenly Father for clarity of mind, strength of heart, and comfort.

When you go through difficult times, do you ask God to help you to lean on Him? Do you ask Him to stand shoulder to shoulder with you in all that you are going through? He will, as the closing Scripture so lovingly reveals. Remember, though, that God does not impose Himself upon us. He wants us to come to Him in prayer. And when we do, like a good parent our heavenly Father will be there.

● ● ● Questions for Discussion:

1. Are you facing a crisis situation or a trying time?

2. Have you asked your heavenly Father to stand with you, shoulder to shoulder, as you prepare to make it through this time?

3. If you're facing such a time, are you willing to turn it over to God in finding the best way to proceed?

4. Besides your heavenly Father, who else can you count on to provide comfort, wisdom, and support in times of crisis, stress, duress, chaos, or grief?

● ● ● Scripture for Reflection: *As a mother comforts her child, so will I comfort you.* —Isaiah 66:13

● ● ● Prayer for Today: *Dear Father, thank You for being with us—always. Please help us to remember that You love us through our trials in life, including our greatest falls. You alone are our source of healing and wholeness. Help us to always be open to Your healing presence in our lives. We love You, Lord.*

10

Happiness Feeds the Heart; Sorrow Opens the Soul

● ● ● Bettie B. Youngs

Our most profound and intimate experience of worship will likely be in our darkest days.

'll never forget the telephone call informing me that my brother's seventeen-year-old son, Aaron, had been involved in an accident while driving to his school's homecoming festivities. Life-flighted to a hospital—where doctors diagnosed the teen's condition as "comatose, severed spine, chances grave"—his stunned parents dropped to their knees, asking God for guidance as their son lay on the brink of death. Obeying God demanded and supported, among other things, moving into their son's room and without ceasing, praying for him, talking to him, reading to him, and singing to him. Nonstop. Not a moment went by without Aaron's being enveloped by love and prayers from family and friends. Fifteen days later, Aaron emerged from his coma, where yet other challenges awaited. Again this family confronted each trial with a *knowing* that God would rule the day in unfolding His plan for their son.

Understandably, the following years were difficult and challenging for this family—in every way. Anytime a promising young person for whom the sky's the limit must suddenly rethink life from wheelchair level is cause to say, "What a tragedy." But times of trial and tribulation can do more than show us our capacity for endurance or resilience: they remind us how fragile we are and show us how much we *need* God. C. S. Lewis once said, "God whispers to us in our pleasure, but shouts to us in our pain." Perhaps he's right. In times of peace and contentment it can seem as though God is almost imperceptible, seemingly silent even though we know He is by our side. Perhaps God is more audible to us in times of distress, heartache, and pain because for all the ways we humans are smart, tough, strong, and noble, in times of heartbreak we discover that self-reliance is not enough. In pain we find a remarkable wisdom: at the depth of sorrow lie the height and strength of our willingness to put our trust in God. Our most profound and intimate experience of worship will likely be in our darkest days. To that end, trials and tribulations serve to alert us, direct us, mold us, and unite us.

Distressing times are, in fact, *fuel* for the soul: while happiness feeds the heart, sorrow opens the soul. Because heartache draws us closer to God, such times are a testimony to the majesty of His love—and so the renewal of courage, hope, faith, and love is possible. In much the same manner whereby an invading grain of sand is transformed into a pearl of great and lasting beauty, the intrusion of difficult times in our lives is an important messenger: tribulation can force us not only to question what brings meaning and purpose to our lives, but to discover the reason for our journey in the first place—to return to Him. As children of the great Creator, no matter how we speak of the mystery, this *is* our universal longing.

Tribulation and heartache are not selective in who they call upon, of course. Inevitably, each of us will face times of sorrow, pain, heartbreak, disappointment, humiliation, or loss. As devastating as such times can seem, we must trust in God to see us through—He has promised to never forsake us. So we reach out to our heavenly Father, asking Him for mercy and comfort as we make our way through our darkest moments—mindful that obedience to His will is the pathway to the bestowal of His blessings.

While it may not seem like it when we are in the thick of distress, all things happen for the good of His plan. This, too, would be true for our Aaron. A few months ago, I attended my nephew's wedding and listened—with a most thankful and joy-filled heart—as Aaron and his high-school sweetheart asked God to bless their lives and their union. Then they thanked Him for His gracious hand in the reconstruction of two lives who found true joy in each other and great purpose in all the ways He'd changed them. And so once again, for these two—and for all who love Aaron so much—God's voice is a gentle, comforting whisper, feeding our hearts with the happiness present in Aaron's new life. But Aaron's story now reminds us not to wait to be buckled by sorrow before we get on our knees before God. In times of sorrow *and* in times of happiness, let our souls be open to God's strong and abiding voice.

● ● ● Questions for Discussion:

1. If heartache or tragedy has already paid a call to your life, how did it change your relationship with God?

2. Do you trust that God has a plan for your life? If so, how is God unfolding that plan?

3. How do we know God is speaking to us, both in times of happiness and times of sorrow?

4. In what ways has happiness fed your heart?

5. In what ways has sorrow opened your soul?

● ● ● Scripture for Reflection: *Consider it pure joy . . . whenever you face trials of many kinds, because you know that the testing of your faith develops perseverance . . . that you may be mature and complete, not lacking anything.* —James 1:2–4

● ● ● **Prayer for Today:** *God, help us to be open to Your voice at all times. Whether You whisper in times of pleasure or shout during our darkest moments, help us to always open our hearts to Your love that we might grasp what it is You are teaching. May the trials of our lives lead us to trust in Your infinite wisdom. Please forgive us when we fail to love ourselves as You love us—and when we fail to love, revere, and trust in You.*

11

How to Know When God Is Talking to You

● ● ● Linda C. Fuller

We can't hear God if our minds are cluttered or if we aren't paying attention—or if our faith is too small to grasp the largeness of God's love for us.

One rainy afternoon, my husband, Millard, and I were driving from our home in Georgia to Florence, South Carolina, to visit our daughter, Faith. I couldn't wait to get there, because this was our first visit with our daughter since she'd started her career in television news broadcasting. So my heart was happy in that respect, yet heavy with personal issues.

I was driving, and Millard was dozing beside me. I knew how tired he was. The past couple of weeks had been some of the most difficult we'd ever been through. The board of directors of Habitat for Humanity International was questioning Millard's leadership style, causing polarization within the organization we had founded fourteen years earlier. Many supported Millard; others were against him. The future seemed uncertain for us . . . much like the weather we were driving through that afternoon. The situation was very upsetting and almost more than I could bear.

Still a couple of hours from Florence, in the silence of the falling rain and the hum of the van, my thoughts began drifting back in time. Themes of rejection, loneliness, and betrayal kept running through my mind. I was overcome with feelings that blended with the sky ahead of me—a sky that became darker and darker as clouds hung low and evening approached.

Don't you just feel helpless, even beaten-down at those times when your emotions move to a dark place? It's like the mother of all soul-searching—which is probably why some call it "the pits." What do you do in times such as these? I used to worry and fret. And then worry and fret some more. But what I've discovered is the most freeing is simply turning the concerns of worrisome times over to God. I can tell you from experience that God has been faithful every time in both hearing me and responding to my heart so full of woes.

On this particular afternoon, I needed reassurance from God—a sign—that everything would turn out all right with this particular crisis. I don't always need a sign, but today, nothing less would do. And then, almost immediately, I heard a voice say, *When you get to Florence, you will see it.* I couldn't believe what I was hearing, so I asked once again. The same voice spoke the same words.

"OK," I said out loud, "I will watch for it."

Suddenly, I noticed a small patch of light on the horizon, directly above the city. As I alternated my attention between the sky and the road, I noticed the light on the cloud was becoming brighter and more elongated, like a column that would hold up a building. Then it took on a pinkish tint, then some green . . . blue . . . and yellow. How incredible: a rainbow! It's a wonder I didn't crash the van—or wake my husband.

I'm sure you've had these moments of "knowing for sure," and this was one of them for me. There wasn't a cell in my body that attributed this *Linda, this is God speaking, and here's the proof you asked for* to chance, luck, or hallucination! Thanksgiving and joy swept through me. God had let me know that everything was going to be all right. My heart heaved a sigh of relief—and like a good daughter, I thanked my heavenly Father for His continued blessings in my life.

The rainbow—it's a beautiful sign, isn't it? The rainbow comes to us as a promise of protection from our heavenly Father, a sign that He will be faithful to us. Its origin was the day God made a covenant with Noah. He put the rainbow in the sky as a sign that He would fulfill the promise He made in Genesis 9:9–17. He vowed that if Noah would build the ark and would do all that God asked of him, then He would never again send a flood to destroy the earth: "This is the sign of the covenant I am making between me and you and every living creature with you, a covenant for all generations to come: I have set my rainbow in the clouds, and it will be the sign of the covenant between me and the earth. Whenever I bring clouds over the earth and the rainbow appears in the clouds, I will remember my covenant between me and you" (Genesis 9:12–15). Imagine, the beautiful rainbow comes to us as a promise of protection from our heavenly Father! And God had just sent this sign to me!

Do you ask God for proof of His guidance and protection over you? You can. From way back in time, we learn of God speaking to us in this way, either in answer to a prayer or to get people's attention. In the book of Exodus, for example, we read that He sent several signs to the Egyptians to convince them that they should free the Israelites from the bonds of slavery. But the Egyptians were slow in listening to God. Each sign from God was a little more "visible" until the Egyptians finally heeded God's commands. So God may send signs as a means of warning, but He also sends them to give us hope—as He did for Noah. And as He did for me.

How about you? Did you ever ask God for a sign? If so, did He deliver? I can tell you from experience that you will never be disappointed when you turn to God for direction and answers. Ask away. The answer may not be something as dramatic as a rainbow (though it could be). It may be a subtle—but sure—feeling, such as, *I know I must [or shouldn't] do this.* Or your sign may come in the form of a sudden invitation to meet a special someone, an unexpected job offer, a visit from an old friend; a long-awaited phone call, or a much-needed apology from someone who once hurt you. However your sign shows up, see it as God's reassurance of His watching over your life. Know that whatever you bring to God in prayer will be answered. But be sure you're listening. We can't hear God if our minds are cluttered or if we aren't paying attention—or if our faith is too small to grasp the largeness of God's love for us.

● ● ● Questions for Discussion:

1. Have you ever asked God to send you a sign? Did He deliver?

2. Why do you think God sends signs to us? What is He trying to tell us?

3. In what way did you thank God for His presence in your life?

● ● ● Scripture for Reflection: *Give me a sign of your goodness because You, O LORD, have helped me and comforted me.* —Psalm 86:17

● ● ● Prayer for Today: *Heavenly Father, thank You for all the ways You prove Your love for me. I am sorry that I am fickle in my faith and that I waver as much as I do. Please help me to learn to listen better so that I might recognize the signs You send to remind me that I am not alone. I love You, Lord. Help me to always make Your will my own.*

12

Turning Fear into Faith

● ● ● Donna Schuller

*What fear holds you back from becoming all that God
has created you to be?*

What are your biggest fears? I have often heard that the two things people fear most are death and public speaking. I can certainly attest to the fear of public speaking, a fear I had even in high school and college. I was the person who always avoided raising my hand. In fact, I tried to sit toward the back of the room and keep my head buried in my book so I wouldn't have to answer any questions. I had to take a public-speaking class in college, but I dropped it because I couldn't imagine delivering a speech in front of a classroom of people! I was very shy and lacked self-confidence, to say the least.

Some years later, I would meet and marry Dr. Robert A. Schuller, a minister who, along with his famous father, had a worldwide ministry. I mean to tell you, if I had known that I would be thrust into the spotlight and in a public-speaking arena, I probably would never have said, "I do"! But that is exactly what happened—beginning on my honeymoon. Robert agreed to a speaking engagement on our trip home from our honeymoon for Amway distributors in Nashville, Tennessee. So here I am, a newlywed—

and the shyest human being in the world—and my husband calls me to the stage in front of thousands of people! All I remember were the bright lights in my face, and I was completely tongue-tied and paralyzed. I could feel my knees knocking, my whole body literally shaking. I remember saying, "Hello, nice to meet you," then scurrying backstage as fast as I could. I kid you not!

Fortunately, God did not allow my fear to go on for too many years. Some fifteen years ago, I was to be the emcee for the International Women's Conference at the Crystal Cathedral. I don't know why I agreed to do this; I guess I felt it was time for me to step up to the plate, and somehow I thought that God would bring me through whatever experiences were to come my way. One of the women I was to introduce that day was Maya Angelou, an incredibly gifted poet and public speaker. As she came into the Green Room where we were all preparing to be escorted up to the platform, I said to her, "Wow, you sure are tall! Your height is deceiving from your pictures." Her response was, "Well, you're not that short yourself!" (I'm six feet tall in heels.) From that point on, I knew we were going to be friends—but little did I know that she was to be the person to help me overcome the fear of public speaking.

As Ms. Angelou and I ventured up the stairway to the platform and waited for our time to go onstage, she looked at me as if she knew and said, "You're afraid. But don't be. I want you to know that you have nothing to be afraid of. You have a lot to offer these people, so you go out there in strength and confidence in the Lord, and you just take over that church." Then she added, "Let's pray." She placed her hands on me, and we prayed. I still remember that powerful prayer. It was a prayer of deliverance from my unrealistic fear of public speaking. I felt the power of God's Holy Spirit surround and strengthen me.

Maya closed the prayer, and I headed toward the platform. I walked onto the stage in front of two thousand women and with total confidence greeted the crowd and introduced the magnificent

Maya Angelou. I was completely and miraculously saved from the fear of public speaking that day. I have never been afraid since. In fact, I look forward to public-speaking opportunities because I love people and believe, as Maya Angelou says, "God will get you through."

What fear is holding you back from becoming all that God has created you to be? For me, it was the fear of public speaking. Once I overcame that unfounded fear, I learned to really enjoy speaking in front of others. And this is exactly what God promises. You see, God has given us a spirit of strength and courage. He tells us to never be afraid. In Isaiah 41:10, we read, "So do not fear, for I am with you; do not be dismayed, for I am your God." God can deliver you from a fear just as He delivered me so many years ago.

It doesn't matter what you're afraid of. It could be a fear of driving, dancing, entertaining, or being alone. It might be a fear of going for your dream or leaving an abusive setting, or it may be a fear of intimacy. Whatever it is, put your trust in God and He will deliver you (and it may be through a friend, as He did for me that day). He will give you the power and the courage you need to face life—and all its challenges. The goal is to keep learning and growing.

● ● ● Questions for Discussion:

1. What fears hold you back?

2. Have you asked for God's help in conquering your fears?

3. Do you have a friend—a real prayer warrior—who can help you pray about what you're afraid of?

4. What step of faith can you take today to help move you closer to overcoming your fears?

5. Do you listen to the Holy Spirit speak to you?

● ● ● Scripture for Reflection: *But you will receive power when the Holy Spirit comes on you; and you will be my witnesses . . . to the ends of the earth.* —Acts 1:8

● ● ● Prayer for Today: *Dear God, open our eyes to those things that hold us back from doing extraordinary things and experiencing the world as You would have us to. Give us faith to believe in Your power to overcome and conquer our fears by opening our hearts to the power of Your Holy Spirit. We trust You with our very lives, Lord.*

13

To Be Loved

● ● ● Bettie B. Youngs

God's love outshines and outlasts any love we will experience here on earth, even though some people here will love us dearly.

One spring day, when I was in the yard planting bulbs, my five-year-old daughter came running over and asked me what I was doing. "Planting gladiolas, honey," I answered.

"Do you like them?" she asked with wide-eyed innocence.

"Oh, yes," I replied, "I love them! They're my favorite flower."

To this she crossed her arms and pouted. "Then I want them to be from me!" she said. Then she sat down and cried.

"Well, then," I said, trying to make her feel a part of things, "whichever ones you hand me, I will believe with all my heart that they were given to me by you!" Only a few bulbs remained to be planted.

A few days later, to my surprise, my little daughter presented me with a gift—a white shoebox on which she had drawn colorful blooming flowers and red hearts. Unable to contain her anticipation of my response to her gift, she put her small hands to her glee-filled face and said in delight, "Now you can say *all* of them are from me!" The box was filled with gladiola bulbs. My daughter had dug up the bulbs I had planted so that when I *re*planted them, they would be from her!

It's been said that receiving love is a human requirement; perhaps giving it is, as well! Certainly the love we give and receive from our children—as well as the other people who own a piece of our hearts—is succor for our souls. But consider that there is even greater love to be had. For all who love us, no one can top the majesty or pureness of God's love for us—including the abiding and unconditional lifelong love of our parents; the romantic and serving love of a soul mate by our sides throughout our lives; and, though difficult to fathom, even greater than the love we parents feel for the children we've birthed. God's love outshines and outlasts any love we will experience here on earth, even though some people here will love us dearly.

God is so serious about His love relationship with humanity that He even protected it by law. In each of the Ten Commandments, God guards something that is of supreme importance to our lives. In the first law He asks that we put Him first in our lives. We are to revere, love, and trust God above all things. By doing this, God is guarding the single most important prized possession we humans will ever have: His love.

In the second commandment, we are explicitly forbidden to make or serve idols of any kind, regardless of what we find attractive, desirable, or honorable. We are to pursue God with the clarity of single-minded focus. Here God is guarding the relationship between Him and us—His children. We are commanded not to place anything—figuratively or literally—before Him. Why? Because doing so would interfere with our knowing and loving God in the way He intends. Anything that comes between God and us could separate us from Him so that we may never understand the real purpose of our lives nor reap the promise His love ensures.

God's love is the most wondrous blessing we could ever hope to have. So enamored with His children, God's love comes with a safeguard. Oh, to be loved like this!

● ● ● Questions for Discussion:

1. How does your love for God surpass even the love you have for your children, spouse, parents, or others?

2. In what ways does God show that His love for you—His child—is even greater than the love you have for your own children?

3. Have there been times in your life when you put your love for someone or something higher than your love for God? If so, what was your life like during this time?

4. How does loving and being loved by God show you the real purpose of your life?

● ● ● Scripture for Reflection: *This is love: not that we loved God, but that he loved us and sent his Son as an atoning sacrifice for our sins.* —1 John 4:10

● ● ● Prayer for Today: *Heavenly Father, You created all things, and by Your will they exist and were created. Thank You for the joys that fill my heart as I acknowledge Your creations—from the flowers I tend in my yard to the love I give and receive from those around me. Teach me to always put You first in everything I do. Truly, I cannot fathom what it would be like to live even one day without Your majestic and all-encompassing love. Thank You for Your great gift of love.*

14

"What Kind of an Outfit Is This?"

● ● ● Linda C. Fuller

You are the only Bible some people ever read.

One day, a man walked by a Habitat for Humanity construction site and asked if he could work. The construction manager was grateful and gave him a nail apron and a hammer. After working about an hour, the man asked, "How much is your hourly wage?" The volunteer working next to him explained that they were all donating their time to build a home for a family in need. Hearing that, the guy put down his hammer, removed his nail apron, and walked away. Before he got too far, though, he turned around and asked, "Does anyone have a cigarette?"

"No," came the reply, "none of us smoke."

The man exclaimed, "You're a bunch of weirdos! You don't smoke and you don't get paid? What kind of an outfit is this, anyway?"

People usually laugh when I tell this story, knowing, of course, that the real weirdo is the man who wandered onto the job site and then decided to go to work without first learning about the conditions of his employment. But the answer to his parting question is that Habitat for Humanity is a nonprofit organization created to help those in need of housing to have a decent and affordable home. These homes are built primarily by volunteers and the future homeowners. No profit is added to the cost of the house, and no interest is charged. This makes the homes affordable to families with limited income.

To qualify, potential homeowners have to meet basic criteria according to need, ability to make monthly mortgage payments, and willingness to put in a certain number of "sweat equity" hours on their home or someone else's. Volunteers work alongside professionals and are thereby afforded a chance to learn construction skills and build friendships with many other like-minded people. It really is an amazing experience to be among a group building a home for someone.

If you've never done it, you really ought to consider it, whether it's on a Habitat for Humanity build or simply assisting someone in your own community to build or repair his home. It's satisfying work and good for your sense of self. We like to think of ourselves as a Christian ministry that puts God's love in action; certainly the many who come to help others get a good sense of what that feels like.

Do you volunteer your time and talents to help others? One of the things I hear most from women is how much they wish they had more time to volunteer. Certainly, when we're caring for young children or aging parents, and should our jobs demand a large portion of our lives, we have limited time. But it's not just the time factor that keeps us from volunteering. Most of us act according to our interests and priorities—so we then treat time differently, don't we? There has to be something to draw us and hold our interest, but the thing is, many women aren't quite sure what that would be. Sometimes you need to try a few things before you discover what that is for you. So it's OK if you join a cause and then decide it's not for you. Don't let that experience stop you from checking out others.

I know that when I was in high school, I had a great desire to be accepted into a social club. Unfortunately, I didn't really have the mind-set for it, but that changed when I was invited to join a Tri-Hi-Y Club, a program for youth in the YMCA. Unlike the social clubs, the Tri-Hi-Y clubs do service projects in the community and build leadership skills. By my senior year, I had become president of my chapter. I realized that this association suited me more and, as it turned out, would prove to develop a really valuable skill in years to come. So think about what interests you, and then think about what you have to offer or what skills you would like to learn. Maybe you're good with people or you have a real knack for organizing things. Or maybe you just want to lend a hand but not be in charge of people or events. A willing heart is all that is needed, so don't be shy. Even if your plate is full right now with family and work obligations, be involved in a cause of your choice, even if your participation is minimal. You'll learn some skills along the way, and you'll gain valuable insight into what interests you.

An even bigger reason to get involved is that sharing your time and talents with others is an enormously satisfying thing to do. It's also a way to "repay" God for His love. God expects us to serve others, as we learn in 1 Peter 4:10: "Each one should use whatever gift he has received to serve others, faithfully administering God's grace in its various forms." And more importantly, volunteering is a way to witness God's love to those around you.

I once saw a sign that said, "*You* are the only Bible some people ever read." How true. People can see and feel evidence of God's love when they see you serving and giving yourself to others. Another favorite quote of mine is by Saint Francis of Assisi: "Proclaim the gospel always and, when necessary, use words." These quotes remind us that "actions speak louder than words." People who may never pick up a Bible have nevertheless come to know God through witnessing His love in action. Never is this more evident than when a Habitat home is completed and we present the family with the keys. We place the new house key on a Bible, and then both the Bible and the key are presented to the new homeowners. When it comes time for the homeowners to speak during the program, most of them first give thanks to God for their answered prayers. And then, with tears streaming down their faces, they thank the staff of the local Habitat affiliate and the many volunteers who came to help them build their dream home. Sometimes it is beyond their comprehension how strangers can give of themselves so generously.

This is the power of helping others. This is the love that is spread when we "serve one another in love" (Galatians 5:13). By helping others, we readily showcase just what kind of an outfit this kingdom of God really is!

● ● ● Questions for Discussion:

1. In what ways are you a volunteer?

2. Why does God direct us to serve others?

3. What step will you take today to start a ministry of service to others?

● ● ● Scripture for Reflection: *I myself am convinced, my brothers, that you yourselves are full of goodness, complete in knowledge and competent to instruct one another.* —Romans 15:14

● ● ● Prayer for Today: *Dear heavenly Father, help me to follow Your instructions to serve other people. I often have an excuse for passing up opportunities to share Your love with others, but I know my reasons are flimsy and not at all in keeping with what You ask of Your children in caring for each other. Fill me with a desire that my actions model well Your love in action. Please show me where my time and talents can be of greatest service to You and those in need—my brothers and sisters on this journey. Thank You for calling us to fulfill Your mission here on earth.*

15

My "Charmed Life"

● ● ● Donna Schuller

There isn't one day that goes by in which God doesn't challenge me to step up to my full potential!

A good friend recently said to me, "Donna, you have the most charmed life!" I smiled and thanked her, not wanting to break her bubble by launching into what I knew would be ten whole minutes of grumbling about how my "charmed life" had *really* been going in recent months. I just didn't have the heart to say, "Well, let me tell you about my charmed life: it begins every day at six, when I get up and make breakfast for my family. Around seven o'clock, the first of a busload of construction workers arrives (so I can forget about lounging around in my robe past seven), all wanting to be greeted with kind words and a smile. All day long, these men are in and out of my house, using my bathrooms and microwave. I am coming up on almost a month of having no desk, books packed away, office papers temporarily 'filed' in the bathroom, bedroom, or my car! But I'm doing pretty well at ignoring all of the rubble, trash, dust, and dirt that is tracked in and out every day by strangers who are hammering, sawing, and creating other auditory disturbances . . ."

Needless to say, in recent months I've been wondering if God isn't giving me an overload of challenges. As I've just described, my family and I have been suffering through this house-remodeling project for the past three years! We are living in our house as the contractors *slowly* complete their various projects (on the days when they actually show up). In the midst of this, the rest of my life must go on. After making breakfast for my family, straightening up the house, and replying to e-mails and letters, I start a couple of loads of laundry. By nine, I begin returning phone calls, set off for the gym, go to my appointments, attend to my community volunteer jobs, check in with my office, and fulfill my duties for the church. And, of course, by day's end, my family expects me to be pleasant and to have prepared all their favorite foods (sound familiar?).

Is your life as "charmed" as mine? If so, then you, too, must have those times when you seriously wonder how much stress you can safely handle before you blow a gasket. I do—I'm always coping with a stress attack. So what I've learned to do is to close my eyes and start listing things for which I am grateful. I find that if I change the focus from all that is wrong to counting my blessings, then equilibrium is restored. It's not a complicated thing; I just start listing all that is good in my life.

So for me, I say things like: *I'm healthy and happy. I have a great husband, healthy kids, and a really close-knit family. I have supportive friends. I love my work. I live in a lovely town in sunny Southern California. My life is both meaningful and purposeful* . . . It's really difficult to continue feeling sorry for yourself when you realize you can make a list and, of course, that it's positive (which is why you list *only* the positive). So then the panic of stress subsides, and I thank God for keeping me in His grace—which I know He does because there isn't one day that goes by in which God doesn't challenge me to step up to my full potential!

But again, as the list of things for which I am grateful fills my mind, I shift gears: I realize that there are many people who don't fret over the mess and chaos of remodeling—because they may not even have a roof over their heads. For many others, life's chores are not about shopping at a grocery store, but about figuring out how to pay for food. And I know that many people can't afford the luxury of working out at a gym—and so on. So, even as stress unfolds around me, I find peace in the eye of the storm. And for this I am grateful as well.

Through the trials and inconvenient situations in life, a wise woman never forgets to recall what is real and lasting in life—what matters most, and what really isn't important in the scheme of things. Pray for the grace to use the stress and pressures of life to help you realize that much of it is because we live in a have-and-have-not world. I have choices when so many do not, so I am motivated to both appreciate and use my gifts and privileges; I've come to see there is much responsibility attached to them. The Bible says it clearly in Luke 12:48: "From everyone who has been given much, much will be demanded; and from the one who has been entrusted with much, much more will be asked." Because I have been so blessed, it is my privilege to thank God, but it is also my duty to use these gifts to make a difference in the world. It is my obligation, a responsibility but not a burden, to help and serve others. I know that God has blessed me with these things so that I might be an instrument for good in the world. Put this way, I realize I truly do lead a "charmed life"!

● ● ● Questions for Discussion:

1. In what ways do you have a charmed life?

2. How do you keep from blowing a gasket when things get overwhelming? Do you ask God for His help?

3. Have you considered that your busy life may be a result of the many blessings you've been given?

4. What responsibilities arise from having a "charmed life"?

● ● ● Scripture for Reflection: *Blessed is the man who does not walk in the counsel of the wicked or stand in the way of sinners or sit in the seat of mockers. But his delight is in the law of the* LORD, *and on his law he meditates day and night. He is like a tree planted by streams of water, which yields its fruit in season and whose leaf does not wither. Whatever he does prospers.* —Psalm 1:1–3

● ● ● Prayer for Today: *Dear Lord, when I become overwhelmed by the chaos in my life, help me to focus on the many blessings I've been given. Despite the stress I feel, I realize that I really do lead a charmed life. Show me how to use these blessings for the greater good of Your people—Your children, my brothers and sisters on this journey.*

16

Do You Ever Feel "Not Enough"?

● ● ● Bettie B. Youngs

The triumph of self-worth is in knowing who we are in Christ.

W hen my daughter was in the seventh grade, she wanted a certain classmate—the most popular girl in class—to spend the night with her. My daughter even went so far as to tell her would-be friend that her parents were good friends with Tom Cruise—and that it just so happened that he would be spending the weekend at our house. The girl agreed to be a guest in our home. Of course, Tom didn't show up, and the white lie was exposed for what it was.

Why did my daughter tell such an outlandish tale? "Because I didn't think that such a popular girl would want to spend time with just me," she later told me, "so I created a reason for her to want to be with me. She was always telling everyone how cool she thought Tom Cruise was, so I fibbed and told her he'd be stopping over. Of course she told everyone at school that Tom Cruise didn't show and that I was probably lying in the first place—so that sort of killed my chances of our ever being friends."

Have you ever doubted your ability to measure up to others— be it your spouse, friends, or even your children—or maybe even *their* spouses and in-laws? Have you ever felt less than others, whether at the office, the gym, or within your professional organization or mothers' group? Sadly, many of us have a little voice inside that says we're not pretty enough, smart enough, wealthy enough, talented enough, or important enough. Why is that?

We all doubt ourselves from time to time. And it definitely feels good when others tell us that we are loving, sociable, bright, and talented! There is nothing wrong with a desire to fit in, with striving to be the best you possible, but self-worth is not up for grabs. All too often we base our worth on how others size up our attractiveness, intelligence, or body shapes and weights. Maybe we base our own self-worth on the same criteria. But when we rely on such an arbitrary and ever-changing barometer, others can make or break us with one word, look, or gesture. How can that be when we are "fearfully and wonderfully made" (Psalm 139:14)? The triumph of self-worth is in knowing who we are in Christ. While self-improvement is always admirable, we must also love ourselves because *we believe* we are "fearfully and wonderfully made." In God's eyes, from the moment you were born, you were already enough.

Self-importance can be a trap. It's a barrier that stands in the way of embracing a humility that allows us to accept God's will for our lives. Our challenge is to rise above feelings of inferiority that keep us from experiencing the fruit of the Spirit. So the next time someone—be it a boss, your husband, your in-laws, or even your own mind—tries to trick you into feeling that you don't measure up, ask yourself in whose eyes must you find favor. Then remind yourself that you must only be enough for God.

As God's heir, created in His own image, you will always be enough. But this too is your work: It's not the responsibility of others to convince you of your good worth. It is your responsibility to believe in the intelligence of the universe, and He who made it so.

● ● ● Questions for Discussion:

1. Do you ever feel as though you're not enough (as in pretty enough or smart enough or interesting enough)?

2. In what ways have you tried to change in order to please someone else, and was this pleasing to you, or did you feel compromised?

3. Do you base your sense of self-worth on your worth to God or how others perceive you? Can you have it both ways?

4. How can your sense of self improve by reminding yourself that you are "fearfully and wonderfully made" in God's own image?

● ● ● Scripture for Reflection: *I praise you because I am fearfully and wonderfully made.* —Psalm 139:14

● ● ● Prayer for Today: *God, I love knowing that I am fearfully and wonderfully made. I take comfort in these strong and positive words. Thank You for loving me that much. Please forgive me when I'm insecure and place too much importance on how others see me. On those times when I need to be reminded that I am good enough, please help me to remember that it is Your assessment of me I am to value most. Thank You for Your patience with me as I strive to grow worthy of Your love.*

17

Are You As Content As God Wants You to Be?

● ● ● Linda C. Fuller

Contentment is God telling us He is pleased.

ecently I was in Indianapolis building a Habitat for Humanity home for a mother and her two children. This family had fallen on hard times, and the mother suffered from clinical depression. (Thankfully, she was receiving medical treatment.) They lived in a dilapidated two-story house in a run-down neighborhood. Nearly three-quarters of her monthly income was consumed in rent for this dump that offered less than substandard living conditions. (Her new Habitat home would require half that amount.)

I had toured the house and was warned not to touch certain light switches because I could get an electrical shock. The stair rail was missing, and in the downstairs bathroom, there was a big hole in the ceiling over the bathtub where waste came down every time the upstairs toilet was flushed. Some of the kitchen flooring was rotten due to chronic plumbing problems. The back door could not be secured properly because the hinges were broken. Can you imagine the stress of living in such a situation? Helping this family build a new home was a total joy, knowing how much it would improve their lives.

As with all Habitat homes, much preplanning goes into any building site before construction commences. Once a "build" begins, each home usually takes anywhere from five or six days to three months to build. Once completed, we do a dedication ceremony where keys and a Bible are presented to the family.

On this particular day, just one day away from the dedication ceremony, I stood back and assessed the progress: sod was being laid; a tool shed was being completed in the backyard; the final coat of paint was being applied to the front porch; and shrubs were being planted. It was a beehive of activity—as was the entire community, since the home we were building for this woman and her family was one of many Habitat homes being constructed in this neighborhood. And then I saw something else that made my heart leap: the street had been named "Carpenter's Circle." Jesus had been a carpenter, and here we were, His "hands and feet"— doing what Jesus would do—helping others.

Finally, the home was complete. All the workers gathered around the house for the dedication ceremony: Habitat for Humanity staff, volunteers, neighbors, and the new homeowner and her family, all standing shoulder to shoulder to rejoice in this new home and to give praises to God for making it so. As usual, the homeowner began to speak, thanking everyone for their love, hard work, and the gift of fellowship. But, her heart so full of thankfulness, the new homeowner broke into tears and was unable to finish her speech. The large crowd of onlookers cheered anyway; she didn't need to say any more. We all knew what this new house, where everything was clean and safe, meant to this family. Then, as the family unlocked the door to their new home and entered it—a symbolic gesture of their being "home"—we all cried.

As I watched the family take that first step inside their newly completed home, once again my heart knew the feeling of contentment—*true* contentment.

Contentment. It's a word rich with meaning, isn't it? We all want to be content, of course, but what brings us to this place of peace in mind, heart, and soul? Perhaps in the early stages of young adulthood, we think of contentment as financial security—having all the things we need, or at least knowing we're on the path toward getting them. We're busy gathering the harvest of our goals: renting or owning a home; buying a car; planning great getaways; paying for education; affording the creature comforts we need, from electronics to wardrobe, and so on. When we start a family, we "gather" even more. Once again we're on a hunt to track down the things we want and need for this stage in our lives. People are great gatherers, aren't they?

Still, having all the things we need doesn't guarantee contentment. Even when we have all that money can buy, many are quick to tell you that no amount of possessions can fill the void of "something still missing" inside. So what can fill this hole we each have? Being right with God is the first source of contentment, of course, and then helping and supporting others. Certainly, we experience a wonderful feeling of contentment after a long day of physical labor—such as being on a Habitat work site from sunup to sundown. And undoubtedly there is great contentment in preparing and having a favorite meal with family and friends. But nothing—other than prayer with the Father—can compare, for me at least, to that feeling of placing the keys on a Bible and handing them to a new Habitat homeowner.

When I'm helping my brothers and sisters in the world in the way that Habitat for Humanity does, I'm content. And I think this feeling of contentment is a sign from God, telling me that He is pleased. When visiting friends, do you find it less a chore to wash someone else's dishes than your own? Or when you are involved in some community service project, don't you find it more fun and fulfilling than a lot of the things you do for yourself? I do. That's because by giving a helping hand to others, we receive joy and contentment for ourselves.

Fortunately, you don't have to quit your job as CEO or policewoman or bank teller to be doing God's work. You don't have to train as a master carpenter, either, to help build a home for others. Instead, you can find contentment by being a "carpenter" for God right where you are. You need only be Jesus' hands and feet in the service of others. No matter what you do—whether it be helping an elderly neighbor rake her yard, delivering a meal to a homebound person, or teaching a child to read—I know that you will find true contentment as you do these things, for we are promised in the Bible, "If they obey and serve him, they will spend . . . their years in contentment" (Job 36:11).

● ● ● Questions for Discussion:

1. Are you as content as God means for you to be?

2. What do you think it would take to bring you greater contentment?

3. What does Jesus' life teach us about contentment?

4. What one thing can you do today that will help another person feel content in her own life?

● ● ● Scripture for Reflection: *You're blessed when you're content with just who you are—no more, no less. That's the moment you find yourselves proud owners of everything that can't be bought.* —Matthew 5:5 MSG

● ● ● Prayer for Today: *Our heavenly Father, I humbly come before You today and ask that You help me uncover and discover contentment in my life. There are so many things tugging on me that blind me to the fact that gathering things is not the path to contentment. Help me to follow Jesus' example in caring for my brothers and sisters around the world. Show me how to be a "carpenter" for Your service. Thank You for teaching us the path to true contentment.*

18

Making Up for Lost Years

● ● ● Bettie B. Youngs

Prayer helps us to lay down the shield we use to protect our-
selves from the hurt that binds us to suffering.

D
o you have a hole in your heart? Are you or have you
been married to someone who never honored your love
or marriage vows? Do you love someone who didn't cherish you? Have you been angry with, bitter toward, or estranged
from your mother, father, sibling, or friend? Did a child get off
track and head down a wrong path? Did you squander precious
time in the grip and daze of addiction, time in which you could
have been more productive—or been a better parent, daughter,
wife, or friend? Has a separation, divorce, or faltered career left
you feeling disoriented and seemingly unable to regroup,
recharge, and begin again?

Many of us grieve for lost and wasted years—times when we
missed out on being productive, joy-filled, and fully engaged in
loving and living life to the max. Worse, we emerge from the fog
filled with guilt and remorse—which in turn can leave us wanting
to crawl back into bed and pull the covers over our heads. Yes, life
happens, but even so, we can get through these times. God promises He will never give us more than we can handle. I saw proof of

this not too long ago when my dear friend, Karen, placed her hand on her father's arm so he could walk her down the aisle. She and her husband were renewing their vows in a formal ceremony on their twentieth wedding anniversary. But the renewal of her vows was more than the love story of Karen and her husband. It was also a victory celebration of having healed an angry heart, one that had been harboring animosity and bitterness for some twenty-seven years.

She had vowed never to forgive him. "I hate him," she once told me. "I despise my father because he loved being an alcoholic more than he loved being a father, and because he caused more bad times than good times for my mother and me. He cheated me out of a father and my son out of a grandfather. He cheated my husband out of a father-in-law. I'm angry because of all the love I wanted and needed and didn't get from him. I'm angry because I wanted to love him, but he wasn't around. I wish I had never known him, because having grown up in a home where he had a presence—but wasn't present—created a hole in my heart so big it can never be healed."

Karen was to learn that God makes good on His promise to restore unto us "lost years." Twenty-plus long years after her father disappeared, Karen received a letter from him, asking if she would forgive him and allow him to make up for lost time. But while Karen missed her father, she didn't know how to forgive him, so for the next three years, the two of them went in and out of some really intense times. Karen pretty much came to the conclusion that, for all they'd worked through, she couldn't completely forgive *and* forget the way he had treated, and cheated, her. Finally she just turned it over to God, asking Him to release her heart from the death grip of the anger she'd been holding on to all these years—and to help her forgive her father for the many transgressions.

Prayer helped Karen understand that while resolution focuses on the problem, reconciliation focuses on the relationship. Resolution means the slate is wiped clean—not some of it, but all of it. It is then that we are able to lay down the shields we use to protect ourselves from the hurt that binds us to suffering. But we cannot possibly lay down our armor on our own. We try, implementing our man-made conflict resolution and effective-communication skills. But forgiving is one thing—forgetting is quite another. Only God can make our hardened hearts ready to receive the salve of forgiveness so that we can heal our wounds and move beyond the paralysis of shame and guilt.

As we learn in 2 Corinthians, "[God] has committed to us the message of reconciliation" (5:19) and "If anyone is in Christ, he is a new creation; the old has gone, the new has come!" (5:17). This is exactly the state of the relationship I saw as a father walked the bride down the aisle—both of them having made up for lost years.

Just as God restored to Karen "the years the locusts [had] eaten" (Joel 2:25), He will restore to you the lost years of love, joy, and productivity. You must only turn your eyes heavenward and ask. Do this. The saying "today is the first day of the rest of your life" is too true to miss out on. Trust God to make your life whole. Trust Him to create for you a new life. In Him, all this is possible.

● ● ● Questions for Discussion:

1. Was there a time when you lost out on being happy or productive?

2. How much time was lost and in what way was it lost?

3. In what way was at least some part a blessing in disguise?

4. Did you find in grieving your loss that this time of despair was, in fact, an occasion during which your prayers were profoundly intimate?

5. In what ways were lost years restored to you?

● ● ● Scripture for Reflection: *"I will repay you for the years the locusts have eaten—the great locust and the young locust, the other locusts and the locust swarm."* —Joel 2:25

● ● ● **Prayer for Today:** *God, teach me to forgive just as You forgive those who transgress against You. So often I am distracted by the joys of life and overwhelmed at the calamities of life. I rely on myself as though I am self-sufficient and can live on my terms and not need You. Still You open Your arms to me. Help me to do the same with my brothers and sisters along the journey of life. Help us all to open our hearts, seeking and granting forgiveness, that we might heal the wounds that keep us from loving one another as You have asked us to. We love You, Lord, and know that all things are made possible through You. We can do nothing without Your love.*

19

Our Sisters' Keepers

● ● ● LInda C. Fuller

Feeling connected to others can bring us into the arms of God.

On the many, many work sites for Habitat for Humanity—whether in Encinitas, California; Manila, Philippines; or Durban, South Africa—one of the things I notice is how willing people are to roll up their sleeves and help other families build a decent house in which to live. And I see how accepting and affirming volunteers are to one another. Granted, we do draw a mixed crowd—young and old alike, men and women, and from every walk of life. Long hair, pink hair, Democrats and Republicans, millionaires and welfare recipients, retired folks and young people, college students and former U.S. presidents, homemakers and First Ladies—all come to work alongside a family in need of a home. But with all their differences, everyone parks judgment at the entrance of the work site.

This seems to be especially true at Women Builds, where all-female crews build the Habitat homes. An example that comes to mind where I became aware of the power women wield when they become their "sisters' keepers," was in Illinois. Here several inmates from a women's correctional facility had come to help.

The heat pump needed to be installed, and nothing more could be done on the house until the heating unit was in place. Arrangements had been made with a heating-and-air specialist to come that morning, but he failed to show up. The site supervisor and the volunteer builders were frustrated until one of the inmates said, "I can install it. It was my work 'before'" (before she was sentenced to time). Everyone looked dumbfounded—but only for about three seconds! "What are we waiting for, then? Let's get to work!"

The woman got the job done by giving directions to her "assistants." When she finally said, "That's it. It's hooked up and ready to go!" everyone clapped, cheered, and hugged their new friend for a job well done. You could see that they genuinely admired this woman for being so knowledgeable and skilled at something the rest of them knew nothing about. With her contribution came even more acceptance. For the rest of the day, others readily included her in chatter as the women went busily about their work, asking her how she was doing, inquiring if she had kids, and so on. She told them she had three children now living with her mother and that she was serving time because she had killed her boyfriend when she discovered that he had embezzled every last cent of her hard-earned money.

Remorseful for her crime and devastated at the lives she'd forever changed, she wept while telling her story. She went on to share how every day in prison was an all-too-real reminder of her crime and of the precious time she'd forfeited by committing it. Her baby, for example, would be twenty years old by the time she was released from prison.

At the end of the day, before the inmates loaded up in their van, they told us how thankful they were to be here, on the work site, doing something constructive, something good for others, and that this was the sort of giving back they could envision as a way to rekindle their own self-respect. We all held hands and prayed together. Then came the real blessing of loving others: the woman who had installed the heating unit invited Christ into her life. After they left, I reflected with the other volunteers that our work that day had given the inmates—all of us, really—the satisfaction of doing good, a sense of belonging, and the warm camaraderie that made a real impression on our hearts. And, by feeling this connectedness, we had brought our new sister in Christ into the arms of God.

Modeling Christ's love for us in our actions is a powerful way to witness. Certainly it was in the love and acceptance of her comrades that this woman saw the hand of God at work—and welcomed Him into her life. This is another reason I so love my work with Habitat: it provides such wonderful opportunities not only to serve others in providing the necessities of life—such as a roof over your head—but it allows us to share our humanness with each other.

On Habitat Builds for women, I see this spirit of sisterhood wherever I go. Women, I see, are especially eager to break through the barriers that threaten to keep us all from experiencing the comforts of life, and the fullness of life. Are you your sisters' keeper? Each and every day, we come across those who are in need of simple praise and acceptance. As my friend Bettie (Youngs) says, "There is no mediocrity of soul" (because to God, each soul has eternal value). May we reach out to sisters everywhere—all of us, God's children—and show for them the love and goodness that is within each of us. Let us remind ourselves that sometimes it takes another person to help us see this for ourselves.

● ● ● Questions for Discussion:

1. In what ways do you witness God's incredible love for your sisters around the world?

2. Are you a witness for God in the way you treat others?

3. In what ways can you be your sisters' keeper?

4. Is there someone with whom you need to share Christ's love and forgiveness?

● ● ● Scripture for Reflection: *Above all, love each other deeply, because love covers over a multitude of sins. Offer hospitality to one another without grumbling. Each one should use whatever gift he has received to serve others, faithfully administering God's grace in its various forms. If anyone speaks, he should do it as one speaking the very words of God. If anyone serves, he should do it with the strength God provides, so that in all things God may be praised through Jesus Christ.* —1 Peter 4:8–11

● ● ● Prayer for Today: *Dear God, forgive me for being judgmental to the point of condemning and separating myself from those who could use my help. By Your Spirit, remind and inspire me to treat others as I would want to be treated. And with the same love and kindness You demonstrated to the woman at the well in Samaria, guide us to do likewise and to give You the praise and glory. Help us, Lord, to always speak Your truth. Convict our hearts when we do wrong and help us to ask forgiveness for our wrongdoings so that we might grow to love and serve others more each day.*

20

A Best Friend . . . Priceless

● ● ● Bettie B. Youngs

*When I am using my relationship with God as a sounding
board for how I direct my life, it is then that I experience the
fullness of His friendship.*

Friends. How could anyone possibly make it through life
without at least one true-blue best friend? Mary Willia and
I became best friends from the moment we met that first
day of college. From that day forward, my life got better. With
Mary as my friend, I was always assured of having someone to sit
with at lunch, college sporting events, or concerts. Always I had
someone to talk to, a sounding board. We did homework together,
discussed our favorite books, and marched in whatever new
protest or rally piqued our interest. We talked about our dreams
for the future and rank ordered (and reordered again and again)
who we thought were the best-looking guys on campus.

Best friends, we were absolutely certain that our secrets were
safe, knowing that we could say anything and the other would not
judge, condemn, or belittle. The moment either of us got in from
a date, we instantly called the other to discuss it ad nauseam. We
laughed together when one of us did something embarrassing or
really stupid, and cried over each other's disappointments and
heartbreaks.

Mary was all things a good friend should be: loyal and someone who really cared about me. She was the first to say, "Way to go!" and the first to feel indignant when I'd been let down. She never let me down. There was not one selfish bone in her body. She wanted the best for me and pushed me out of the nest at those times when I didn't have the same level of confidence in myself that she did. In short, with Mary as my friend, I was a better, wiser, and more compassionate person than I would otherwise be.

Many years have passed, and still she is my dear friend. When our lives get too crazy or when the weight of the world begins to feel like a burden too heavy to shoulder—or at those times when we simply wish to revisit the "girl within"—we get together. The secret to the friendship between Mary and me is the high level of care we give to preserving what is special between us. We are right with each other. Not all friendships are this solid, of course. Sometimes friendships wither away from a lack of attention, and sometimes they die to the toxicity of sabotage or betrayal. Sometimes we fail to do those things that solicit others to take a chance at being our friends—which is a lonely place to be.

Wouldn't it be wonderful if we all had many good and perfect friends? Some of us do, and some of us do not. But whether we have many friends or a few good friends, we each have a perfect Friend: His name is Jesus. And one of the greatest blessings of being right with God is knowing that He is by our side, rejoicing at our victories and soothing our hearts when they're bruised. He knows our past and present, and yet . . . He will never desert us.

Like my good friend, who supports, encourages, and cheers me on, Jesus, too, does all that. But though He is a faithful friend, He is not a passive presence. Always He asks excellence of me, continually whittling away my rough edges so as to turn me into an effective servant-leader for Him. Keep in mind that God made us expressly for a relationship with Him. When I am using my relationship with God as a sounding board for how I direct my life, it is then that I experience the fullness of His friendship. What an awesome knowing.

● ● ● Questions for Discussion:

1. In what ways does the relationship you have with a best friend mirror your relationship with God—and vice versa?

2. Friendship is a two-way street. In what ways does God have a friend in you?

3. Is friendship with God automatic, or does it require specific actions on your part?

4. In what ways does God mold and grow you to be a better witness for Him?

● ● ● Scripture for Reflection: *You are my friends if you do what I command. I no longer call you servants, because a servant does not know his master's business. Instead, I have called you friends, for everything that I learned from my Father I have made known to you.* —John 15:14–15

● ● ● Prayer for Today: *Dear Lord Jesus, thank You for the gift of friendship and for those people I've been honored to call friend. And thank You, truly, for being my Friend in all ways. You are always faithful and always there for me. You are with me in all my feelings, and You fill me with peace that really does surpass all understanding. Thank You for Your love and for the knowledge that I can always count on and trust in You. Thank You for showing me in Your Word how to be a friend.*

21

The Essence of Prayer

● ● ● LInda C. Fuller

Thank You, Jesus.

World-renowned evangelist and author Tony Campolo once told me about something that happened when he was a guest speaker at a church. He was coming to the end of his sermon when he noticed a small boy in one of the pews aiming a crayon at the head of a woman seated in front of him. Obviously, the boy had become bored and was contemplating turning his crayon into a projectile! His father, caught up in what Tony was saying, didn't notice what was happening until the boy let the crayon fly. The woman quickly turned around and gave the boy a mean look. Dr. Campolo said it was difficult for him to keep his mind focused on what he was saying, especially when he saw the father take the boy by the hand and head toward the back. Then, in a voice that everyone could hear, the little boy pleaded, "Please, everybody, pray for me!" Obviously, we are never too young to pray or to ask others to pray for us!

This example is humorous (perhaps not for the little boy), but it brings to mind a serious question: do you come to God regularly in prayer? I guess how you answer that depends upon what you believe about the importance and power of prayer. For example, maybe you think that prayer takes time, so you put it off until you have a bigger window of time. But prayer needn't be a long, drawn-out affair, and we can even pray anywhere, anytime. We can pray for (or with) our children while taking them to school. Donna (Schuller) says that when someone is talking to her, if she senses the person is struggling with an issue, she silently prays for that person while listening to her. So prayer is simply calling God into the picture.

One of my favorite Scripture passages shows Jesus teaching us *how* to pray:

> And when you pray, do not be like the hypocrites, for they love to pray standing in the synagogues and on the street corners to be seen by men. I tell you the truth, they have received their reward in full. But when you pray, go into your room, close the door and pray to your Father, who is unseen. Then your Father, who sees what is done in secret, will reward you. And when you pray, do not keep on babbling like pagans, for they think they will be heard because of their many words. Do not be like them, for your Father knows what you need before you ask him. (Matthew 6:5–8)

What comes next in the Bible text is what we call the Lord's Prayer. At times when I am short on words or too upset to think straight, I know that I can always start off by praying the Lord's Prayer. It stands alone or sets the tone for a continuing conversation with God about any specific concerns.

In the Scripture passage I quoted above, I especially like the suggestion about going into your room and closing the door to pray. However, I don't think we need to take that literally. What I think Jesus means here is to pray in any private and quiet place.

For example, I feel close to God when I am on a sandy beach at sunrise, on a mountaintop, or surrounded by trees in a forest.

Of course, we can't always be in these beautiful and inspirational settings when we pray. At times we pray at a bedside, holding the hand of a loved one who is ill, or at a Habitat construction site with a fellow volunteer who is troubled. Did you know that you can even pray with someone on the telephone? The first time someone did that with me, I was somewhat amused, because I had only heard people praying in church, so this method seemed a little unholy. But as I thought about it, I could see where this way would be perfectly acceptable to God. No matter where we are, God's Spirit is right there, and we can talk as well as listen to Him.

As you may know, Habitat for Humanity's mission is to provide affordable homes to families in need, but we also pride ourselves in doing God's work. We say that every house we build is a sermon of God's love. And prayer is a huge part of how we determine what and where and why we do what we do. Since the very beginning of Habitat for Humanity in 1976, we have always started each workday at our headquarters in Americus, Georgia, by taking turns reading a passage of Scripture, sharing a story or something in a spiritual vein, and then closing with prayer. On construction sites we do the same thing before putting on our tool belts. And when a house is completed, the keys and a Bible are presented to the new owners at a house dedication ceremony. It's a joyous occasion when lots of people give praise to God and all the people who worked on the house. We open and close the program with prayer, and then people tour the house and have refreshments.

Probably the shortest prayer I know is "Thank You, Jesus." Martin Luther once said, "The fewer words, the better prayer." I remember seeing the power of these words when a new Habitat homeowner in Georgia was seeing her beautiful finished house for the first time. Walking into the living room of her new home, she looked around and said, "Thank You, Jesus." She then went into the kitchen and, observing all the beautiful cabinets, said, "Thank You, Jesus." Next she went into her freshly painted bedroom and said, "Thank You, Jesus." Finally, she came to her sparkling bathroom and said louder than before, *"Thank You, Jesus!"*

As her heart was full and she was praising the Lord, she reached down and turned on the hot water in the bathtub. It looked so inviting that she immediately locked the door, stripped down, and got in for a soak. As the divine heat from the warm water penetrated her body, she just repeated over and over, "Thank You, Jesus. Thank You, Jesus. Thank You, Jesus." She told us later that this was the first time she had ever bathed in a tub. Well, just as this grateful woman was thanking God for this blessing of a hot tub bath, which so many of us take for granted, we can express appreciation to God for our blessings too.

We sometimes forget that prayer is *two-way* communication. In fact, prayer is *the most important conversation we will have each day.* Through prayer, we can speak to God; we can ask others to pray *for* us and *with* us; and, most importantly, we can listen for God's messages *to* us. Have you ever participated in a prayer group or chain? If you have, then you understand the power this can bring to those in prayer, and especially to those being prayed for. Scores of people have prayed for me during times of crisis, and I know it works. "Therefore confess your sins to each other and pray for each other so that you may be healed. The prayer of a righteous man [and woman] is powerful and effective" (James 5:16).

So pray. Nothing is more powerful than calling God to you— and asking Him to bless others as we start our days. I love these words by John Bunyan: "He who runs from God in the morning will scarcely find Him the rest of the day." Start your day out right—with a prayer. No matter how early you rise, you need never worry about waking the Lord! He'd love to start His day with you, too.

● ● ● Questions for Discussion:

1. Do you have a special place and time for prayer each day?

2. What events in your life prompt you to talk with your heavenly Father?

3. Have you received answers to your prayers?

4. Have you participated in a prayer group or chain? Why do you think they are so powerful?

5. Have you prayed yet today?

● ● ● Scripture for Reflection: *I pray that out of his glorious riches he may strengthen you with power through his Spirit in your inner being, so that Christ may dwell in your hearts through faith. And I pray that you, being rooted and established in love, may have power, together with all the saints, to grasp how wide and long and high and deep is the love of Christ, and to know this love that surpasses knowledge—that you may be filled to the measure of all the fullness of God. Now to him who is able to do immeasurably more than all we ask or imagine, according to his power that is at work within us, to him be glory in the church and in Christ Jesus throughout all generations, for ever and ever! Amen.* —Ephesians 3:16–21

● ● ● Prayer for Today: *Dear Lord, I confess that I don't spend enough time talking to You and even less time listening, because I am so busy with my life. We are so blessed to be able to come to You in prayer whenever we wish. Please keep me mindful of Your presence. Thank You for always listening to—and answering—our prayers.*

22

Beyond an Intellectual Faith

● ● ● Bettie B. Youngs

The storms of life can buckle our lives—
and if our faith is merely an intellectual-level one, they will.

There is a lovely parable of a delicate little bird who found shelter every day in the withered branches of a dried-up old tree in the middle of a deserted plain. One day a whirlwind uprooted the tree, so the tiny bird was forced to fly miles and miles in search of shelter. The journey was long and tiring, but fruitful: the little bird came upon a lush forest, full of fruit-laden trees.

Like the dust storm that forced the little bird to search deeper, experiences that shake, rock, and otherwise threaten to buckle our lives can move us beyond business as usual and, instead, to search out a new place—a new way—to live. Whether our angst causes us to reel, scream, plead, or cry out to God, one thing is for certain: when we go knocking—or kicking, screaming, or banging—at God's door, we do find God. As with all productive fights, the exchange leads us to a new understanding of ourselves and beyond a mere intellectual-level understanding of the God of the universe. The difference of the distance we've then traveled is not just a matter of degree, but of redo—much like when a house burns down.

It is not about remodeling but, rather, rebuilding, as Wayne Dosick discovered when a wildfire burned his house to the ground. Standing before the ashes and charred remains of what had been their home, the Dosicks held each other, numb, unable to say anything except the whispered sounds of their disbelief. Those ashes had once been their dream house, and their loss was compounded by the fact that both worked out of their home. Wayne was a rabbi, writer, and professor. Ellen, a psychotherapist, saw her clients and conducted workshops and seminars in a section of the house she specifically designed with this in mind. Now they had lost their home and all their personal valuables, as well as their offices and all their professional assets.

"How much is the Hermitage in St. Petersburg, Russia, worth?" a reporter once asked a guard at the palatial, world-famous museum. "It's impossible to ever know," came the response. That's exactly how the Dosicks felt as they took inventory of all that had been lost. There were the six thousand volumes in Wayne's rabbinic library, including the Hebrew Bible—a historic treasure that had been saved from the fire of the Holocaust, but not from an indiscriminate California wildfire.

There were irreplaceable mementos: all the photos of their children growing up, special occasions, birthdays, and awards ceremonies. The hundred-year-old grand piano, every sermon Wayne had ever written, Ellen's client records, tapes of radio shows, financial records, and legal documents . . . all forever gone. But the fire did more than destroy their home and possessions and devastate their businesses. From coming to grips with their loss to helping and supporting each other as they grieved separately—and differently—the couple discovered that the fire had also seared a hole in their marriage—a marriage they thought could weather anything. In dealing with damage the fire had wrought, there were moments when they weren't so sure their marriage could survive it.

Their soul-searching during this time must have been incredible. Consider for a moment Wayne, a man of God, his very life dedicated to his faith. Can you imagine the talks he must have had with God? Like the fire that completely devoured everything in its wake, his very faith had been tested to its core. In dealing with all he'd lost, he sought comfort from God, but railed against Him too. He begged God for mercy and, at the same time, accused Him of not sparing a man who was His servant. Oh yes, Wayne and God had words on more than one occasion! Little did he know that such discussions would force him to rebuild his sense of God from the ground up. But much like the little bird whose strife pushed him into finding a land of lush trees, Wayne arrived at a far richer place than he could ever have predicted. The branches of his earlier faith withered in comparison.

A faith once rooted in his intellectual and professional life had been tested mightily, and the result was a greater breadth and depth and scope of God than he had ever known. Now Wayne would do more than talk with his congregation about trusting God when times were uncertain. He now knew God intimately and could speak to others on a level he never even understood, much less had a capacity for, before his own faith had literally undergone trial by fire.

Like the homeless little bird, we, too, will have our own whirlwinds that uproot our lives—whether divorces, unemployment, broken hearts, addiction, financially hard times, accidents, terminal illnesses, or simply the feeling of a never-ending despondency. All shake us up, holding the potential to break us—and if our faith is merely an intellectual-level one, they will. If our relationship with God is one that essentially says, "Don't contact me; if and when I need You, I'll contact You," then when the storms of life blow in, we'll no doubt blame God or, worse, renounce Him.

Some storms are more destructive than others. Perhaps these are the most important ones to God, for they most assuredly present an opportunity to rebuild not just the material things we have lost, but also our relationships with Him. In this, the storms of life are productive in that they move us from an intellectual understanding of God to a deeper and richer relationship with Him. But we need not wait for a "fire" to drive us into a rich and lush relationship with the Almighty. We can do this even when the sun is shining and the skies are clear.

● ● ● Questions for Discussion:

1. In what ways has a whirlwind shaken up your life?

2. How did this affect your relationship with God?

3. Is your faith rooted in an intellectual understanding, or do you personally know God?

4. Does God intentionally send trials our way so as to test us?

● ● ● Scripture for Reflection: *From its chamber comes the whirlwind . . . the clouds scatter his lightning. They turn round and round by his guidance, to accomplish all that he commands them on the face of the habitable world. Whether for correction, or for his land, or for love, he causes it to happen . . . stop and consider the wondrous works of God.* —Job 37:9–14 NRSV

● ● ● Prayer for Today: *Dear heavenly Father, I know that I am all too easily disarmed and disoriented with the calamities of life. But I know that You have plans for my life and that fires and whirlwinds are sometimes necessary to get me to move to a new place of living my life for You. Forgive me for worrying about cleaning up the ashes instead of thanking You for helping me to seek the lush forest—that place where I will come to know You intimately, to build a relationship with You that will transform my life so that I might have life everlasting. Your love is so great! Thank You for standing by me in the trials of life. Please help me to always ask what it is You wish for me to do, and give me the humility to obey when You point me in the direction You wish me to go. I choose You. I choose to rebuild my life upon You, my Rock and my Redeemer.*

23

The Turkey Exchange

● ● ● Donna Schuller

When your best-laid plans collapse, look for the blessings it brings.

Most of us really cherish family gatherings during the holidays. If your family is like mine, you have certain traditions that you respect and follow every year. At my house, holidays for the most part are fairly predictable: special family recipes are shared, cherished stories are retold, relationships are rekindled, and, in some cases, new traditions begin.

But holidays can also be times loaded with stress, especially if our best-laid plans threaten to collapse. As I've learned, in such times you simply need to adapt as best you can and then look for the blessings it brings. This was the case for our family one Thanksgiving several years ago. My husband, kids, and I decided to spend a nontraditional Thanksgiving aboard a small fishing boat anchored off the beach in Baja, California. As with every year, I wanted this to be a memorable and perfect holiday for my family—so I was a little bit tense about our change in plans. Everything had to be precisely choreographed so that we could make the best use of the small space—and even smaller oven!

Weeks ahead of time, we made lists that included the measurement of the oven, the pots and pans available, etc. Upon close scrutiny, we decided that the oven would accommodate only an eight-pound turkey, which would be quite a change from our usual twenty-two- to twenty-five-pounder. About two weeks prior to the trip, I found a great price on an eight-pound turkey, and I tossed it in the Deepfreeze. About the same time, my mother called and wanted to know if we had room in our Deepfreeze to store a twenty-two-pound turkey for her. She was planning on having guests for Thanksgiving dinner and needed a turkey bigger than her freezer could hold. "No problem," I told her. "I have plenty of room."

So we prepared for our trip. My very helpful husband always packs the cooler for all of our family outings—it's just one of the jobs he likes to do. So while I was helping the kids get their bags closed up, Robert loaded the turkey into its "cold box" for our trip, and off we went. Well, you can imagine my surprise when, at our destination, I opened the ice chest to find a *huge* turkey staring back at me! Robert had inadvertently taken my mother's turkey! I screamed at him to come and explain why he'd done such a stupid thing. Poor Robert didn't know that my mother had stored her turkey in our freezer. His defense was that when he looked in the Deepfreeze, he only saw one thing that looked like a *real* turkey to him . . . so that was the one he took! This didn't make any sense to me, because we'd discussed the size of the turkey weeks ago. But to Robert, it just did not compute that a small eight-pound turkey would actually look more like a frozen chicken. He had taken what looked to him like a turkey.

Well, after panicking and acting like a turkey with a butcher at his tail feathers—and after leaving a panic-stricken and apologetic voice message for my mom via cell phone—I finally calmed down. And, of course, we had a really good laugh about it all and prayed that my mother would hear the voice message in time to shop for a new turkey. I did feel really terrible about flying off the handle, but really, who doesn't get stressed out by the holidays, especially when you want everything to be perfect?

Well, you know what? Our Thanksgivings weren't ruined after all. My possibility-thinking husband creatively butchered the turkey so as to fill our small, eight-pound roasting pan beautifully. We gave the rest of the bird to a local family nearby, and they were very happy about it—because, as it turned out, it was to be their only taste of turkey on Thanksgiving! And it worked out OK for my mother, as well, because her dinner plans changed and her company did not come. We had a lot to thank God for on that Thanksgiving Day. Truth be told, there were blessings enough to go around—blessings of sharing, blessings of new acquaintances—as we gave away our extra turkey to another family. And it was all made possible by the unexpected "turkey exchange"! No one could have planned it better than, of course, our Father, the Grantor of all blessings.

There's a Yiddish proverb that says, "Man plans, God laughs." (Of course, that's true for women, too!) I like to imagine God holding His breath, just waiting for Donna to explode when she discovered that enormous turkey instead of the one she'd been expecting! As this situation taught me, God always has a way of making our mishaps work out somehow. I should have remembered this when I blew up at poor Robert! When things don't go as we think they should . . . when our holiday plans get messed up . . . when people don't do the things we think they should do, we need to keep in mind that God is in charge, and if we trust in Him, He will help us through. In this case, my family survived—even thrived—and had a wonderful Thanksgiving after all, even if it didn't go exactly as I had planned.

Remember this the next time you make a cake for the school bake sale—and your son drops it on the floor. Remember this when you get to your vacation destination—and discover your luggage was shipped someplace else. Remember this when you're racing to make an appointment—and your car battery picks the same day to die. Stay calm. Ask God to show you the wisdom in your situation—and ask Him to let you be pleased with the surprise blessings it brings (like my "turkey exchange"). And learn to laugh when things go wrong—which I have to tell you, we've done so many times since that day.

● ● ● Questions for Discussion:
1. Can you recall an occasion when things did not go according to your plans?

2. How did God bless you and show you ways to appreciate your situation?

3. When best-laid plans go awry, what lessons can they teach us?

● ● ● Scripture for Reflection: *And we know that in all things God works for the good of those who love him, who have been called according to his purpose.* —Romans 8:28

● ● ● Prayer for Today: *Dear God, thank You for sometimes changing our best-laid plans, even when we think they are set in stone. You are an awesome God, and You always work things out for our own good—even if we don't understand it at the time! Help us to handle these situations with a sense of humor and a spirit of calm, keeping ourselves open to the lesson that You would have us learn.*

24

The Single Most Important Thing You'll Ever Teach Your Child

● ● ● Bettie B. Youngs

Ask God to protect your children, yes—
but the real protection lies in the fact that they know God.

Whether our kids are five or thirty-five, today's headlines give us many reasons to be concerned for their well-being: Will they have to fight in a war? Will they be tempted to drink or use drugs? Will they succumb to an eating disorder? Will they be injured, killed by a drunk driver, or fall victim to a hate crime? We live in precarious times; danger seemingly lurks everywhere. A good friend who has two teenagers and has just had twins told me that she was watching TV a few weeks ago when an Amber Alert interrupted the program. A young girl was missing. The next day the child was found; she had been abducted and killed by a man with a long criminal record. The child was only eleven—the same age as one of my friend's own sons.

Every day as she takes her son to school, she passes a little wooden cross by the side of the road. It's the site where a fourteen-year-old boy was killed by a car as he crossed the street on his bicycle. This little boy was the same age as her oldest son. "I can't help but think that if it can happen to that child, it could happen to my own," she told me. Both of her sons are at ages when they are longing for more independence. "My head tells me this is normal," she says, trying to rationalize her need to protect them and yet not frighten them. "But my heart is full of fears for their safety. 'Don't talk to strangers,' I'll tell them for the thousandth time. Or, 'Be careful crossing the street.' I utter a prayer every time they walk out of the house alone, hoping for their safe return."

Certainly in these times we need to be on high alert for all the ways harm can run across the paths of our children. And yet, an unreasonable fear for children implies that we're not trusting God to look out for our loved ones. Yes, our instinct is to pull them close and never let them out of our sight. But God, too, is their protector. God assures us of this. As we learn in Matthew 18:10, God has even assigned special angels to watch over children: "For I tell you that their angels in heaven always see the face of my Father in heaven." Yet for all of God's protection, sometimes children are still harmed or even die. We know that God is always with us in our suffering, and that we should "rejoice in our sufferings, because . . . suffering produces perseverance; perseverance, character; and character, hope" (Romans 5:3–4)—but this is hardly salve for the hearts of those parents who have lost a child to disease, starvation, drugs, or a bullet. And so we are left staring fear in the face and asking God what He would have us do with it.

What *shall* we do with it? We can begin by asking—and answering—a most important question: What will happen if I die tomorrow? The answer, found in Hebrews 9:27, is that we will stand before the judgment seat of God. There will be those who have never put their trust in Him—they will suffer eternal separation from God. And there will be those who have said, "I have placed my trust and faith in Him." These will spend eternity with God the Father in heaven. Can you say that if you died right now, you would know for certain that you have eternal life? The same question applies to your children. Ask yourself, *if anything should happen to my child, can I rest in the peace of knowing my child now has the promise of eternal life?* In other words, *do my children know God personally?*

Teaching our children about God's love is the single most important thing we will teach them. Ask God to protect your children, yes—but the real protection lies in the fact that *they* know God. Ask God to put a hedge of protection around your children, yes, but do not neglect to teach your children the love of God, their heavenly Father. When we teach our children how to have a personal relationship with God, we can be at peace, knowing that our beloved children will forever journey in God's kingdom. Do this for them. And then believe with all your heart that our Father will watch over your children as He has promised in Exodus 23:20: "I am sending an angel ahead of you to guard you along the way."

● ● ● Questions for Discussion:

1. How has being mindful of your children's safety produced a new consciousness and a willingness to be more active in the world to ensure safety for others?

2. When your worries for your children overwhelm you, do you turn them over to God?

3. Do you trust that God has a plan for your children and is looking out for them even as danger abounds in our world?

4. Do each of your children know God?

5. How has the reality of living in a more dangerous world caused you to turn your eyes heavenward and to call upon God to keep your children—and others throughout the world—safe?

● ● ● Scripture for Reflection: *But let all who take refuge in you be glad; let them ever sing for joy. Spread your protection over them, that those who love your name may rejoice in you. For surely, O LORD, you bless the righteous; you surround them with your favor as with a shield.* —Psalm 5:11–12

● ● ● **Prayer for Today:** *Father, I know You are the greatest Father of all and that You love my children even more than I do. I am so grateful. Thank You for Your blessings, and for hearing so many of my 911 calls over the years in the name of my children. I pray that You would protect all children the world over, Father—for these, too, are Your own.*

25

Trusting God More

● ● ● Linda C. Fuller

Isn't that just like us humans? We ask God for something, and then we don't trust He'll deliver.

had tons of work to do on this book. My friend and coauthor Bettie was saying, "Linda, I need your material ASAP"—as my dentist was strongly recommending that I have a wisdom tooth extracted. My reaction was, "Oh, no! I'm going to be down and out for a few days, and it's going to put us behind!" Bettie and I joked about it, too, because I made the remark that of *all* the times when I could be writing stories for a book entitled *Woman to Woman Wisdom,* it happened to be when I needed all the wisdom I could get! But my appointment was set. So I said to God, "Please help me through this, because we're doing Your work here in writing this book, so any help on the healing part would be appreciated!" And you know what? Now that I've had the surgery, I'm feeling great! It's a blessing from God. I haven't had any pain whatsoever, even though I took a couple of painkillers to play it safe. I think we could say "hurrah" to God—and give a little credit to my dentist too!

Isn't that just like us humans? We ask God for something but then don't trust that He'll deliver. But why bother consulting God if we don't heed His advice? Why bother calling upon God to help us out if we fail to trust that He'll see us through it? Bettie shared with me about a recent conversation she had during brunch at a friend's house. A man seated next to her said, "I was so lonely and had been divorced for a long time. Finally one day I just prayed, 'God, please bring me my beloved. I so much want to love someone.' And you know what? You'll never in a million, kazillion years believe it, but the very next day I met this woman, and she's been my wife now for three years! And we are both so in love and happy that we have found each other." This man had no doubt that God would bring him his heart's desire—and He did!

One of my favorite heroines of the entire Bible is Ruth. Her bravery and trust inspire me still. She had the spirit and faith of a true pioneer. Ruth was born and raised in the country of Moab, and she married one of Naomi and Elimelech's sons. (They had fled Bethlehem, Judah, when there was a famine.) After some years, Elimelech and both of his sons died. That left Naomi and her two daughters-in-law all widows.

After a time, Naomi decided to return to her birthplace, but she encouraged the other two women to stay in their home country of Moab. The one widow quickly decided that she certainly didn't want to move to a strange country where she didn't know anyone, but Ruth was determined and insisted on going with Naomi, even though neither of them knew who would support them now that they didn't have husbands. But Ruth was unafraid. She told Naomi, "Where you go I will go, and where you stay I will stay. Your people will be my people and your God my God" (Ruth 1:16).

As it turned out, God blessed Ruth's decision, because Naomi happened to have a fairly wealthy "relative on her husband's side . . . a man of standing, whose name was Boaz" (Ruth 2:1). He fell in love with Ruth, and he took her to be his wife. They had a child named Obed, who became an ancestor of David, one of the most famous kings of Israel, not to mention, in the line of Christ Himself. Just think, if Ruth had not trusted God to take care of her, it could have changed the whole course of Hebrew history! We never heard David speak of his great-grandmother Ruth, but one could say that a lot of her courage and trust in God were passed on to him. Remember when he volunteered to slay that pesky Philistine giant (1 Samuel 17)? That's another incredible story of faith and trust in God.

There are many other wonderful examples in the Bible of people who dared to do the seemingly impossible because of their trust in God. Noah continued building the ark that God told him to make, even though his friends were making fun of him. Abraham trusted God enough to leave his homeland and most of his belongings to travel hundreds of miles for many years for the purpose of establishing God's presence on earth. Then there was shy, stuttering Moses, who obeyed God's command to confront the great Egyptian pharaoh and demand that he let the Hebrew slaves go free. Moses then led them across the desert for forty years to find the "land . . . [of] milk and honey" (Deuteronomy 11:9).

Well, having a wisdom tooth pulled doesn't compare with these powerful stories from the Bible, but all of these circumstances nevertheless show that each one of us has many opportunities during our lifetimes to be either timid or bold. Have you had times when you dreaded something and you prayed to God to help you through it—but then you were surprised when He did exactly that? Why do we not trust that God will be there for us? I think so many of our dreads and fears are unfounded. We are naturally afraid of what we don't know or haven't experienced before unless someone who has been through it helps waylay some of our fears.

How do you respond when you're required to take a leap of courage? Do you rise to the occasion, or do you step back because you have trouble trusting God? Do you hold back on scheduling that necessary surgery because you're afraid of the outcome? Do you hesitate to change careers because you might jeopardize your financial security? Do you turn down the job offer in another state because you fear you'll be lonely? Do you put off calling an old acquaintance because you fear rejection? Are you unwilling to stop drinking for fear you can't "be you" without the crutch of chemicals?

If your doubts and fears are holding you back, you need to hand them over to God. The Bible tells us, "Do not fear, for I am with you; do not be dismayed, for I am your God. I will strengthen you and help you; I will uphold you with my righteous right hand" (Isaiah 41:10). Think about something you've dreaded or been afraid to do. Then say to yourself, *I trust in God. He will see me through this.* When you trust in God instead of going it alone, you will be properly equipped to handle anything . . . including writing a book, or cruising through wisdom-tooth surgery when you haven't one minute to lose!

● ● ● Questions for Discussion:

1. Do you ever feel that you're too timid and wish you were braver about doing new things?

2. What specific thing have you been putting off because you're afraid of the outcome?

3. Do you understand how holding back can indicate a lack of trust in God?

4. Do you believe that God will be with you if you do something that you're afraid to do?

5. What first step will you take to bring yourself closer to confronting your fears and trusting in God?

● ● ● Scripture for Reflection: *"Be strong and courageous. Do not be terrified; do not be discouraged, for the* Lord *your God will be with you wherever you go."* —Joshua 1:9

● ● ● Prayer for Today: *Our Creator in heaven, how we marvel at how You have accomplished amazing acts by Your people through history! May these stories inspire us to have the same trust in You when we are confronted with something we're reluctant to do. Thank You for always being there for us when we are afraid. Please remind us of Your presence when our fears creep up on us. Please help us to trust in You.*

26

Are You As Fun As You Should Be?

● ● ● Donna Schuller

We're to smile and laugh and act as though we're genuinely happy to be alive.

Are you a serious sort of person? I have a tendency to be that way. When I am involved in a project or task for which I am responsible, I tend to get really intense. Yet I don't want to lose sight of the need to enjoy every moment or to "stop and smell the roses" along the way. Can you relate? It can be easy to get so wrapped up in our roles as mother, wife, employee, employer, and citizen of the human race that we forget how important it is to have fun (a lot of fun!) along the way. This is really true for me, because, especially in my role as a pastor's wife, I take my life very seriously. This is good, of course, but still I know there are times when I just need to lighten up.

Luckily, I have a good friend who models what I need to learn—to incorporate laughter and fun into daily life. My friend's name is Mary. She is truly a fun person to be around. Thoughtful, intelligent, caring, truly loving, and with such a quick wit—Mary has learned the art of seeing life through the eyes of fun. She's just the perfect example of someone who can roll with the punches.

Thanks to Mary, I've relocated the fun and carefree girl within

myself. She gives me the courage to bring out the joy and spon-
taneity that most of us so closely guard once we become adults.
Never is this more true than when the two of us go to get our nails
done. Nothing can be more fun than going for a manicure with
Mary. As you've probably experienced, the mood in most nail
salons is rather solemn. Well, when Mary and I go into a salon, we
change that! One day, she and I were getting our nails done
together, and upon hearing the Beatles' tune "Imagine," we started
singing. At the top of our lungs, we sang—and not necessarily on
key! Now, you can imagine how singing out loud in a salon is
going to get some strange looks—and most people will think
you're either crazy or you've forgotten to take your medication.
But that's not what happened this time. The lady to my left, genuinely entertained, broke out in a belly laugh and thanked us for
taking her mind off her stressful day. And the salon operators were
so amused that they started chattering merrily among themselves
in their native language. We couldn't understand their language,
but that made us laugh even more.

Yes, I know this all sounds a little goofy and not the most serious example of fun—I mean, it doesn't compare with a ski trip or
a European tour. Still, a dose of lighthearted fun can remind us
that fun is also within our repertoire of emotions. We are meant to
have fun. And our lives are meant to be fun: we're to smile and
laugh and act as though we're genuinely happy to be alive and
truly blessed to have been given the time we're each allowed.

I encourage you to find your own "Mary"—or better yet,
become one—and build fun and laughter into your life. Find a
way to lighten up your life on a daily basis. In fact, the Bible tells
us that we should conduct ourselves with happy hearts. "All the
days of the oppressed are wretched, but the cheerful heart has a
continual feast" (Proverbs 15:15). Why do you think God wants
us to experience happiness and joy? Because, as we learn in
Proverbs 15:30, "a cheerful look brings joy to the heart."

Our happiness and joy show that we take delight in the

wonderful world that God has given us. Make today a happy day. Wear your happiness and joy on your face. The result will be a blessing to others. If you're having a hard time getting into the swing of this, start by calling a fun-loving friend, like Mary, and ask her to meet you for some laughs. Rejoice in this beautiful day the Lord has made!

● ● ● Questions for Discussion:

1. Are you too intense or more serious than you'd like to be?

2. Do you have any friends who help you see the lighter side of life?

3. Why do you think God wants us to lighten up?

4. What are the benefits of being joyous and playful? How does it affect those around you?

5. What one thing do you plan to do this week to have more fun?

● ● ● Scripture for Reflection: *May the righteous be glad and rejoice before God; may they be happy and joyful.* —Psalm 68:3

● ● ● Prayer for Today: *Dear Father, during those times when I start to get a little too serious, please help me to lighten up and learn to smell the roses that You have placed in our lives. Please lead me to people who see the joy in life, and help me to be a positive, happy influence on others. Thank You for this beautiful world that You have created for us to enjoy.*

27

Goals—In What Way Is God Growing You?

●●● Bettie B. Youngs

God was keeping my Day-Timer—I just didn't know it.

've always been a great goal setter. For a long time I attributed this to my early years—namely, wanting to move beyond them. I grew up in a large family in rural Iowa, where the most likely progression after high school was to get married and raise a family—in other words, to repeat and perpetuate more or less the same journey I'd seen. As honorable as that is, I wanted nothing of it. In my senior year of high school, when all my friends rushed to get engaged—and the boy I was dating suggested we go look at diamond rings—I was terrified, realizing I'd better get working on an escape plan. So I got really serious about going to college—purposely *not* applying to any that were within driving range of my home community. It was a time of much prayer.

Young, energetic, and with a fistful of goals, off I went. Accomplishing these goals, I discovered, was a snap. I attributed their achievement to, first of all, *having* goals and, secondly, to putting my energy behind them. That made sense: cause and effect. So off I went, the world being but an oyster to me. By the age of twenty-eight, I had years of teaching school under my belt (even being named Teacher of the Year), along with a master's degree and two doctorates, both from accredited institutions. I had married and had a child.

By age thirty, I'd searched out enough opportunities so as to travel and lecture in some fifteen countries, and I'd landed a position as the first woman to be named to a graduate teaching post in a large university. Again, off I went, happy and even more energized. In all this time, I'm not sure that I was ever consciously aware that I was driven or that I was moving at breakneck speed: it all seemed really natural and easy to me. "If only there could be more hours in a day," I'd say. There were so many more things I wanted to do.

I no longer naively believe that my drive to "go" and "do" was my own doing. God was keeping my Day-Timer—I just didn't know it. Looking back, I'm absolutely sure that the goals I set and achieved had little to do with my wants but, rather, were simply a part of His plan for me. Having grown up in a Christian home with a loving and magnificent mother, who not only fervently prayed for her family but also consecrated our lives to God, I know now that God laid claim to my life early on. He even kept me in His grasp when I ran off into the waiting arms of the world without even saying, "See you later." Young and spirited, I've no doubt God watched, perhaps chuckling at my oblivion, letting me run around the world and work off some energy, all the while seasoning me for what was yet to come.

I realize now that in all my activity, God was growing me, showing me that the faith my mother lived was worth claiming as my own. Certainly, the people I met and worked alongside over the years were doing God's work and not at all bashful about giving all glory to God for everything in their lives. I was showered with acceptance and fairly quickly moved into positions of responsibility where I was stretched into the next level of learning, growing, and changing.

Being young and full of myself, I assumed my acceptance and

achievement were because I had a good work ethic, liked people, and, of course, deserved it. Obviously, I know better now. I see all as having been the hand of God at work. A little smarter, I've no doubt that through the years God has been preparing me, maturing me to witness and to minister—and in the way He intends me to. It is my honor to open my heart and stand prepared to obey. I accept that I am to serve and glorify God in all that I do. It is time for me to take my place in the world as someone who is not simply taking from it, but sharing what I have learned by being groomed by others who count themselves among His dutiful servants.

So though my calendar is as busy, I know that it is God who opens doors to me—I let *Him* be in charge of which ones I'm to go through. Whatever His plan, I know that I am not the message; I am only the messenger. As such, whenever I feel a tugging at my heart that won't go away or an ambition or drive that refuses to go unmet, I recognize it as belonging to Him. And so I have bowed my life to Him, saying, as in Psalm 143:10, "Teach me to do your will, for you are my God." And though I still wish there were more hours in a day, there is not a moment that passes for which I am not grateful for God's love and for the plan He has for me.

I am so thankful He has ownership of my soul—and for a mother who taught me who made it so. Slowly but surely, I am becoming a wiser woman.

● ● ● Questions for Discussion:

1. In what ways are your goals a part of God's plan in preparing you for a larger truth?

2. In what ways are the passions in your heart the voice of God?

3. How is God working through others to prepare you to come to Him?

4. In what ways are you creating for family, for friends, and others you meet along the way a love for God?

● ● ● Scripture for Reflection: *I press on toward the goal to win the prize for which God has called me heavenward in Christ Jesus.* —Philippians 3:14

● ● ● Prayer for Today: *Heavenly Father, may the passions in my heart belong to You. All that I desire, Lord, may it be to Your glory. Help me to recognize those times when Your hand is guiding me and to choose the right path to You. Let me be Your messenger in all that I do. Teach me to do Your will. I want my work—and life—to be pleasing to You, Father. Guide me, that all I do might glorify You.*

28

Are You Chasing the Wind?

● ● ● Bettie B. Youngs

How can the miracle of meaning, purpose, and direction find you?

The phrase "Live each day as if it were your last" makes for a nice saying, but how many of us take it literally? When my friend Nancy Rivard's father unexpectedly died at the age of fifty-six, the phrase took on a sudden urgency for her. "He was still so young," she told me, and added, "That life can be so unpredictable and can be taken from you in the blink of an eye is more than disconcerting; it's scary."

With a new respect for "life is short," Nancy began to take stock of her own. She started by taking a look at people around her, especially friends and work associates. She concluded that they were all "nice, good, hardworking people," but missing a certain spark of what she called, "zest, zeal, and genuine happiness." Assessing her social circle, she found them to be "an interesting, fast-moving, and fun group, who were never at a loss for excitement" and yet, the appeal for her was gone. Examining her own situation, she discovered that, though continually busy, there was no great passion of purpose going on. "Sometimes I feel as though I'm just going through the motions," she said, "chasing the wind.

I'm busy all the time, but to what end? Losing Dad is a reminder that our years aren't guaranteed. I need a purpose. I want my life to have greater meaning."

And so she began her search to find it. She resigned from her more time-consuming administrative/supervisory position with the airlines and took a position as a flight attendant so she'd have more time and freedom to do the things she'd always wanted to do but never got around to. She went back to school to pursue doctoral studies, spent time with family and close friends, and attended workshops and conferences. She journeyed to the four corners of the earth—from the U.S. to Tibet, from the Philippines to El Salvador—you name it; she was there.

And then one day, magic happened and great clarity arrived: "I want my life to revolve around serving others," she declared. This seemed a bit nebulous, so she asked, "OK, God, how am I to do that? Like, what am I to do?" Recognition was instant. *See a need, and do what you can to help,* came the response to her heart. "I remember standing there, holding this discussion—out loud—with God, thinking those around me must have thought I was a crazy woman!" she said, laughing. "But the clarity kept coming."

Nancy realized that everything she needed to serve was already in place! Possibility after possibility after possibility came tumbling out of her head. And so she began. Using her connections with the airlines, Nancy began by searching out orphanages and delivering humanitarian aid and goodwill everywhere her company's route took her. She escorted orphans from one end of the world to new homes in another. She solicited organization after organization, asking for everything from medical supplies to food, clothes, and toys for orphaned kids. She pleaded with doctors and other experts to travel and help others for free. Year after year after year.

Nancy was no longer chasing the wind—now she was chasing a passion that gripped her and wouldn't let go. Not that she wanted it to: "It's an awesome way to live," she tells everyone. "Whether this is my last day on earth or the first of a hundred to come, I'm smack in the center of a passion-driven life filled with purpose and tons of fun. If I were to die tomorrow, this is exactly how I am to live today."

Can you say the same? Are you chasing the wind? Is your life lacking passion and purpose? Maybe you feel bored with life or tired of your current lifestyle. Perhaps you feel as though one day passes into the next, but that none is necessarily fun or worthwhile. How can you change that—how can the miracle of meaning, purpose, and direction find you? For each of us the answer is different, but we must begin the search in the same way: by asking God to beam a spotlight on the path to living a glorious life, one that revolves around His will for our lives. The result will be clarity of purpose, renewed energy, and a happiness of heart that is real and pure.

Certainly this has been true for Nancy Rivard. Today, the outreach of Nancy's service to God has spawned Airline Ambassadors—a nonprofit organization that touches the lives of literally millions of people via its efforts to deliver humanitarian aid and medical services to those in need the world over. Every day of her life is filled with serving God, bringing glory to Him. And every day, God's children are served because this courageous and most loving woman so desired to discover the mission of God's will for her life. May we all uncover the courage to get in sync with God's will for our lives.

● ● ● Questions for Discussion:

1. Have you ever felt that you were chasing the wind, perhaps lacking purpose in your life or feeling an emptiness inside?

2. Do you have a thirsty spirit but have never considered that God could quench it?

3. How would your life be different if you asked God to be Lord of your life?

4. Are you keeping your distance from God because you're afraid of how your life might change if you ask Him to help you discover His will for your life?

● ● ● Scripture for Reflection: *I undertook great projects: I built houses for myself and planted vineyards . . . I bought male and female slaves . . . I also owned more herds and flocks . . . I amassed silver and gold for myself, and the treasure of kings and provinces . . . I refused my heart no pleasure . . . Yet when I surveyed all that my hands had done and what I had toiled to achieve, everything was meaningless, a chasing after the wind; nothing was gained under the sun.* —Ecclesiastes 2:4–11

● ● ● Prayer for Today: *God, please help me to live my life filled with passion and purpose. During those times when I feel as though I am chasing the wind, help me to turn to You and ask, "Lord, what is it that You wish for me to do with my life? What is the purpose for which I was created?" Teach me how to make Your will my own. Fill me with Your Holy Spirit, Lord, that I might love You as You created me to.*

29

Do You Have a Guardian Angel?

● ● ● Bettie B. Youngs

None of our problems come without God's permission.

As a young child, over my bed hung an old, old picture of a young girl lying in bed, saying her prayers, with two angels hovering near the head of her bed. I was always struck by their seemingly different roles. One angel is watching the child, listening intently to her prayers. The other angel's beautiful and peace-filled face is seen from the side, and her head is raised heavenward. She has one hand placed across her heart and the other hand outstretched, as though beseeching God to hear the little girl's prayers. I so loved this picture. It always made me feel safe and protected. No boogeymen dared come for me in my room.

Several years ago, when my daughter was going through a rough spot in her life and hanging out with a couple of boogeymen friends from, it seemed to me, planets yet undiscovered—and hopefully will remain that way—the angel picture once again showed its power. As I lay awake one night, my beloved child heavy on my heart, I asked God to deliver her from these friends. But God informed me that what I saw as mistakes she was making were decisions she was choosing. Yes, consequences might very well be severe, but none of our problems come without God's permission. I wanted to retrieve my child pronto, but God was telling me to calm down. This was not what I wanted to hear.

I continued to lean on God for her to begin seeing things my way. But while God heard from me day in and day out, it seemed to me that most of my prayers went unanswered—until in the wee hours of one particularly restless night, I awoke to an idea that seemed more like a command: *Hang the angel picture above her bed.*

Brilliant, I remember thinking. *Why haven't I thought of that?* So up I got; I drove to her apartment and hung the picture of the beautiful angels above her bed.

A few days later, she called and said, "Thanks for that," and went on about her life with these menacing friends. Distraught and upset at her misuse of her time and talents with an unseemly lot of lost souls, I went again to her apartment, this time to remove the picture, as if to say, "If this is the lifestyle you're choosing, I'm taking my angels back!" My fury was compounded when I found that she had relegated the picture to a closet in another room!

Then, a couple of weeks later, my daughter drew a line in the sand and stepped over—cleaning house of all her lost friends. She went to a minister she loves and requested to be baptized. Having made herself new in God's eyes, she stepped forward into a new day and time—and with a newly cleansed soul. Simple as that.

"What was the moment of that decision?" I later asked her. "Well," she said, "when you hung the picture of the beautiful angels over my bed, I could hardly sleep there. I took them down and put them in the closet, because it was too painful to see my lifestyle and then see the innocence and protective love just flowing out from these angels. It made me feel so unworthy. But even stashing them in the closet in the next room didn't diminish their effect on me. And then one day, I couldn't 'feel' them, so I went to the closet and, sure enough, you'd taken the picture back. That was upsetting. At first I felt humiliated, but then humility set in: I felt that your removing it from my apartment meant that you didn't consider me worthy of the angels' love and protection—and maybe even yours. I couldn't bear the thought."

The spirit of the angels had done their job, reminding my daughter of God's love. As my daughter said, "It was time to honor my Father's call—which, by the way, Mom, I don't think I would have gotten around to nearly as soon as I did without my having lived on, as you call it, 'the other side of the moon' for a while."

Do you believe in angels? Have you ever wondered if you have encountered one? Do you know if a guardian angel has been assigned to watch over you? Angels are fascinating to contemplate, aren't they? There are many descriptions of angels, as well as their various duties, documented in the Bible.

Angels are messengers of God who deliver news to people on earth, as did the angel Gabriel when he announced to Mary that she was to be the mother of Jesus (Luke 1:26–38). But the primary role of angels is to administer aid and comfort to people in times of need. They visited Jesus after His forty days of fasting and temptation by Satan in the desert, prior to beginning His formal ministry (Matthew 4:11). They were with Him at other times, too, including in Gethsemane, as He prayed before His arrest and crucifixion (Luke 22:43).

Angels are sometimes referred to in Scripture as "the heavenly host" who worship and serve God in heaven. The word *host* implies that they exist in vast numbers. Many stories testify to the fact that angelic beings have rescued people from imminent danger. And we learn in Hebrews 1:14 that angels are "spirits sent from God to care for those who will receive salvation" (NLT). An angel went before Israel's army, guaranteeing their victory. Another shut the mouths of the lions for Daniel. Still another opened prison doors for Peter, saving his life on the eve of his execution. An angel also showed up in a storm to let Paul know that he'd be OK. And an angel spoke to my daughter, convincing her it was time to return to a life of walking hand in hand with God.

Be open to the grace of angels. If you're going through a tough time of your own, it might comfort you to find your own angel picture—or pin or figurine—and place it where it will always remind you that God's angels are watching over you. If a friend or family member appears to be lost, pray for that person, asking God to put a shield of protection around her and to send His "angel power" to work in her life, as He so promises in Psalm 91:11 (NLT): "He orders his angels to protect you wherever you go." And above all, heed the wisdom in this prophetic Scripture: "Don't forget to show hospitality to strangers, for some who have done this have entertained angels without realizing it!" (Hebrews 13:2 NLT). Oh, the wondrous love of our heavenly Father!

● ● ● Questions for Discussion:

1. Have you ever felt the hand of an angel at work in your life?

2. Do you feel God has assigned a guardian angel to watch over you?

3. Do you believe that our loved ones in heaven get assigned as an angel by God to look over those of us still on earth?

4. What should we teach our children about angels?

● ● ● Scripture for Reflection: *I am sending an angel ahead of you to guard you along the way.* —Exodus 23:20

● ● ● Prayer for Today: *God, it is so comforting to know that Your angels can come to earth to protect us, reveal Your truths, or intervene with love on Your behalf. Help me to recognize those times when I need an angel's hand and to enable Your angels to work in my life. I know that guardian angels are one of Your gifts to us—further evidence of Your enormous love for us, Your children. Thank You, Lord, for Your great love.*

30

The Truth Behind a Rotten Day

● ● ● Linda C. Fuller

When bad things happen, laugh—then "do battle."

Have you ever gone through a time when one thing after another in your life seemed to be falling apart? It happened to me just recently. First, there was a serious power struggle within the ranks of Habitat for Humanity International leadership. This was a time when Habitat was experiencing an explosion of growth and an abundance of resources pouring in. Sadly, there were divisions, squabbles, and lots of hurt feelings— abundant distractions from our overall purpose to eradicate substandard housing.

If the stress from this wasn't enough, my personal life seemed to have a chain reaction—sort of like dominoes falling—of its own. For example, one day while driving, suddenly I saw a dead deer in the road! There was no way to avoid this big heap of carnage without swerving into oncoming traffic, so I ran right over it. Immediately, I could smell a potent and sickening odor. This horrible smell literally clung to my car, and whenever I drove it, I had to tolerate this awful stench. Right around that same time, a male cat got inside our car and decided to claim it as his territory by "marking" it. I had the car sanitized three times, but still, both unpleasant odors—from the dead deer *and* the territorial cat— remained for months!

Then my dryer went out, and with my schedule, getting a replacement and being home for its delivery were extremely inconvenient. Every day that was suggested was bad for me. "No, I'm in Africa that week . . . No, that week won't work either. We're in Michigan and then leave for Uganda for three weeks." Stress! Shortly thereafter, I was rearranging my work area at home, so proud of myself for finally getting around to purchasing new shelving to organize my supplies. The shelves were square, stainless steel grids held together with black plastic sprockets. I stacked several sets together, making four cubicles high and four cubicles wide. Everything fit perfectly. All was well until I started removing a box I had placed in one of the bottom cubicles. It was like the tumbling of a house of cards. My printer broke that day, too, giving real meaning to "the straw that broke the camel's back." It was just one thing after another!

I was talking to a friend about all this, and she suggested that I might be under attack. I thought about her comment and realized she was right. Do you believe that times like these are just a string of bad luck, or could they be the work of an evil force attacking you? As uncomfortable as it may be to discuss, evil forces do exist among us, as Scripture confirms: "Jesus said . . . 'Satan has asked to sift you as wheat'" (Luke 22:31), and "Be self-controlled and alert. Your enemy the devil prowls around like a roaring lion looking for someone to devour" (1 Peter 5:8). Yes, good people and good works are being attacked at every level, the goal being for them to lose hope and to not trust that God's hand is upon them.

So do not be deceived by the work of evil forces in your life and in the world. But do more than just understand this reality: do all you can to ward off the forces of evil thrust upon you. When you're going through a time that feels like the dominoes are falling, ask friends and family to pray for you. Enlist prayer chains, which are also powerful voices to pray on your behalf.

And here's something else you can do when bad things are happening: rather than being fearful or upset, smile and say as I do, "It's just the devil up to his mean tricks again!" When you do this, something amazing and productive happens: the stranglehold upon you is broken—just as we are promised: "Submit yourselves, then, to God. Resist the devil, and he will flee from you" (James 4:7).

The Spirit of Christ is more powerful than evil. Evil may get its moments, but Christ's Spirit will be the victor. The next time a series of bad things happens, laugh—then do battle by remaining strong in your faith and through prayer. If you do this, you'll never have to say, "The devil made me do it."

● ● ● Questions for Discussion:

1. Have there been times in your life when it seemed as if everything was going wrong, like a wall of shelves falling down?

2. Do you attribute these times to just bad luck, or have you considered that it might be an evil force at work?

3. Do you have a special friend or people in your community you can depend on for prayer?

4. What can you do on a daily basis to strengthen yourself and your loved ones against the force of evil?

● ● ● Scripture for Reflection: *Put on the full armor of God so that you can take your stand against the devil's schemes.* —Ephesians 6:11

● ● ● Prayer for Today: *Dear Father, when bad things happen to me, draw near and keep me mindful that Your power is greater than any other. Keep me safe and surround me with Your protection as I struggle to remain faithful to Your calling for my life. Help me to resist the forces of evil and to draw strength from You.*

31

What Is Your Favorite Song?

● ● ● Bettie B. Youngs

Christian music delivers our hearts into the presence of God.

A couple of months ago, my daughter and her boyfriend took me to the airport. A very beautiful CD by a Christian artist was playing, and when a particular song came on, both sang along with full-on abandon! I was fascinated by this and especially enjoyed being privy to the joy they were experiencing. Having been relegated to the backseat, I took notice of the case of CDs nearby and looked through it. Only Christian artists were in the music collection. My daughter's boyfriend noticed my finding and remarked, "It's all Jen and I listen to. We find the beauty and inspiration of Christian music really centers our relationship." Then, laughing, he added, "Plus, it's tough to argue or be upset when you're listening to it. Should either of us be feeling a little short with the other, the music reminds us to ask ourselves what Jesus would do in this situation. Right away we're back focused on God's love—and our own."

I was impressed, of course, and thankful that my daughter was with such a smart guy. And I was reminded of the beauty and power of Christian music to keep our hearts and minds joyous and centered on God's love. I saw this with my mother. She was always singing and humming, constantly praising a most loving God through song. An unforgettable memory is seeing the joy in her face when she sang what I'm sure was her favorite song, "In the Garden." The words say, "I come to the garden alone, while the dew is still on the roses . . . and He walks with me and He talks with me, and He tells me I am His own." I was sure she believed the message of this song with all her heart, and singing the words helped her feel it and thus know it. It was a rich experience to live with a mother who felt so powerfully loved by God; to her, music was a medium of God's love.

Do you have a favorite Christian song, and have you considered why the words bring joy and happiness to your heart? My favorite is "How Great Thou Art." When I hear it, my heart just melts, surrendering to the knowledge that I am loved by such an omnipotent Power. For me, the lyrics move me into the feelings I have when I'm face-to-face with a miracle—such as the moment I saw my newborn for the first time. I even have a favorite voice from whom I prefer to hear this song: George Beverly Shea, who sang it for many years when he toured with Rev. Billy Graham.

I'll never forget the first time I actually saw Mr. Shea sing this song. I was ten. First came the voice booming from the television, and then, when I saw him, there was this very tremendous hulk of hugely handsome man. I was sure that Mr. Shea *was* God, simply here on earth masquerading as a great singer!

Though many thought Mr. Shea wrote the song, he didn't. It was written in 1885 by a twenty-six-year-old Swedish minister, Carl Boberg, who composed the song over time. The first verse was written when Boberg was caught in a thunderstorm in a Carpathian village; the second as he heard birds sing near the Romanian border; and the third as he witnessed many of the Carpathian mountain dwellers coming to Christ. The final verse was inspired by his travels in Great Britain.

The song had a long and mysterious journey before it came to the public's attention. During the 1954 Billy Graham Crusade, Mr. Shea was handed the song on a napkin by someone in the audience.

He sang it, and the rest is history! During the 1957 New York Crusade, Mr. Shea sang it ninety-nine times. It was simply stunning—especially when the choir joined him in the majestic refrain "Then sings my soul, my Savior God, to Thee! How great Thou art! How great Thou art!"

How great Thou art. What phrase has more power? What words could ring more true? They certainly express our love for our Lord. I encourage you also to "come before him with thanksgiving and extol him with music and song" (Psalm 95:2). Berthold Auerbach once said that "music washes away from the soul the dust of everyday life." Certainly, music does just that. But it does more than help us to reach beyond trying times or the daily routines of life. Christian music can deliver our hearts into the presence of God so that we desire with all our hearts to know the greatness of our Creator.

● ● ● Questions for Discussion:

1. Do you praise the Lord with singing?

2. What are some of your favorite Christian songs? Why do they have special meaning to you?

3. Have you shared Christian music with a friend, especially someone who is in need of inspiration?

4. Do you use Christian music to remind you of God's love and readiness to walk with you through troubled times as well as to appreciate moments when all is right in your life?

● ● ● Scripture for Reflection: *Speak to one another with psalms, hymns and spiritual songs. Sing and make music in your heart to the Lord.* —Ephesians 5:19

● ● ● Prayer for Today: *Dear Father, What a wondrous gift You have given to us—the sound of music! Thank You for Carl Boberg and the great Bev Shea and for all those whose gifts of music, through You, help lift our spirits, inspire our thoughts, and turn our hearts to You. May the gift of music we choose always reflect Your greatness and move us closer to You, dear Father.*

32

Little Old Ladies

● ● ● Donna Schuller

Do you ever wonder about what your life will be like
when you're a very old lady?

've just returned from visiting my beloved ninety-eight-year-old grandmother. She is wonderful and a real survivor. I just love her! Certainly, she's taken good care of herself, but she has also practiced the art of rolling with the punches. One of the keys to living a long, full, and happy life is to adapt to change, and my grandmother has done just that. We should all be so wise: for women, the need to adapt is especially important because our lives so often revolve around others—and who knows what path that's going to lead us down?

Deaf since childhood, my grandmother relied on a hearing aid and lip-reading in her early years, but as she got older and her vision faded, she lost her ability to read lips. Although she could still get her point across verbally, she had a hard time comprehending my responses. I finally resorted to writing my communication out in bold black letters on a tablet. When she and I were together, we'd each have a pad of paper and get caught up on things in this way. But eventually that, too, became frustrating for her. So then we moved on to other means of sharing time—and life—together.

One day I took her out for a long walk in her wheelchair. As we were returning to her assisted-living center, we passed by the back entrance to her previous independent residence. Grandma had lived there with her husband for more than ten years until his death, so I was worried that going by this spot would dredge up too many painful memories. But being there did not weigh heavy on her heart: Grandma talked about the beauty of the flowers, the cars in the carports, the birds in the air. While the thoughts of my beloved grandmother having to revisit these memories made me sad, they seemed not to affect her in this way. Grandma, I realized, had learned to live in the moment—and appreciate all that it was. My grandmother is a great adapter; she has learned to adapt to the continually changing circumstances in her life.

Not me! I found myself crying, wishing I could turn back the hands of time. I recalled how my grandmother had lived in her house for so many years, surrounded by the things she had accumulated over the course of her lifetime. But when she moved into a single room in an assisted-living facility, it meant leaving some things—well, *many* things—behind. And so our family has had to disperse most of her belongings. How difficult this is to do for someone you know and love. It is simply heart wrenching. I couldn't fathom what it must feel like to her. So now, aside from a few photos, several changes of clothes, and a few small pieces of furniture, she has no material belongings to show for her long and productive life.

So as I wheeled my grandma past this site, I thought about how sad it must be to lose everything—including nearly everyone she's known throughout the years. I took stock of who she has lost: her own father and a little brother to the flu of 1917; my father, her only son, died in a car accident when she was sixty-three; her mother died soon after her son; one of her older sisters recently died; and, of course, she has lost many friends and other loved ones over the years. I cry for her, but also for me.

I'm all too aware that in little more than a year from now, I will be fifty years old. I take note of the fact that my grandmother was fifty when I was born. This makes me wonder what my life will hold in the future. Do you ever wonder about what your life will be like when you're a very old lady? As a woman with nearly fifty years of life under my belt, I don't know how many days my dear grandma has left or, for that matter, how many days God has in store for me. I only know that I have a better chance of living happily if I'm adaptable—if I adapt to the changes in my life instead of holding on to regret for life's passing. Even the experts agree, saying that one of the characteristics of longevity is the ability to roll with the punches. Those who accept and embrace change—and don't allow themselves to be overwhelmed or dwell too long on sorrow—experience more years and better health than those who cannot adapt in these ways.

Perhaps, as my grandmother has discovered, if we're too busy looking back, we won't see the wonderful things that God has placed upon the path we're walking here and now! Grandma can appreciate God's beautiful flowers and birds today because she is grateful for her past *but will not sacrifice* her present. I pray that with wisdom and love I will continue to face each day as it comes. As we are told in Ecclesiastes 7:14, "a man cannot discover anything about his future." Only God knows my future, and I will trust that with His help I can handle whatever it holds. In the meantime, let us love, respect, and care for our elderly family members. And keep in mind that each "little old lady" in the world is our mother, too.

● ● ● Questions for Discussion:

1. Do you adapt well to change, or do you have a hard time adjusting?

2. Why is the skill of adapting especially important for women to acquire?

3. How can your faith in God help you to "roll with the punches" of life?

4. Do you consider all "little old ladies" your grandmother, too?

● ● ● **Scripture for Reflection:** *Rise in the presence of the aged, show respect for the elderly and revere your God.* —Leviticus 19:32

● ● ● **Prayer for Today:** *Dear heavenly Protector, life can be filled with adversity and sorrow, and sometimes I find it difficult to overcome these times. Help me to trust that You can help me through whatever life brings my way and to learn to adapt to the changes that inevitably will occur. Instead of looking toward the end of my life with dread, anticipating its uncertainties, help me to embrace what comes my way with peace, knowing that my life is in Your hands. Thank You for our grandmothers, and through them showing us the value of time, and that in the end, it is all about returning to our heavenly home.*

33

Why God Created Chocolate

● ● ● Bettie B. Youngs

Living with a man is an exercise in perfecting our own nature. God is putting us to the test: Do we deserve chocolate, or not?

Whenever my mother was exasperated with my father, she'd mutter (loud enough for him to hear), "God may have made Adam first, but He took one look and said, 'Surely I can do better than this!' Hence, woman—the better, finer, and wiser of the two!" As a child, I so loved my mother's feistiness; as an adult, I've gained a whole new appreciation for her considerable intellect. Not that I don't love men. I mean, what would life be like without them? Children need not spend their entire waking hours trying to frustrate us; we have men for that! Of course, men do have their redeeming qualities—and we can talk about those at a later date. But for now, let's focus on why God created chocolate.

We all know that the primary reason God made chocolate is because it's His way of apologizing to women for the goof-up of using dust in His creation of man (instead of using DNA—as He did in the creation of woman). God is well aware that creating Adam from dust explains why many of men's shortcomings frustrate women.

Take selective memory, for example. Ask any man what team won the first Super Bowl, and he'll tell you that Green Bay defeated Kansas City in 1969. And if you really want to test his memory, try asking him who won the first World Series. Don't be surprised when he tells you it was the Boston Red Sox in 1903. But ask any man the date of his wedding anniversary, and you'd think you were asking him to read your mind or nurse the newborn! *I hope he doesn't forget my birthday,* we tell ourselves as we look at the calendar and wonder how we can drop a subtle but effective hint that it (or our anniversary) is but days away—hoping that his silence on the topic means he's already done his shopping. We anticipate a special piece of jewelry, a new outfit, or other heartfelt gifts, but realistically we know that a vacuum cleaner or a food processor is more likely. Why are men so practical, anyway?

And then there's the matter of inattentiveness. Remember when you first started dating? Chances are he brought you roses "just because." He probably called you several times a day just to say hello. Maybe he gave up watching his football game to go shopping with you. But now that you're a bona fide couple, well, you can't remember the last time you smelled roses in the house. He doesn't call unless his taste buds are savoring the idea of a little something special he'd like you to whip up for his dinner. And he wouldn't even consider turning off the football game to run errands with you. Let's face it: once the ring is on your finger, the courting usually comes to a screeching halt. Luckily, when God installed the Romance gene in man (which was downsized due to the space needed for the hefty Sports gene), He didn't toss it out altogether—as He did with the Honey-You-Just-Relax-While-I-Make-You-Dinner gene.

The list of annoyances is endless, of course, but space is limited. So what are women to do? Most women suffer in silence. *He doesn't pay attention to me anymore,* they tell themselves. *He takes me for granted.* Or worse, in their hearts they worry that he no longer loves them with the same passion as when they first started dating. *I've put on a few pounds*, they fret. *He's no longer attracted to me.* But instead of getting too neurotic, we need to understand that living with a man is an exercise in perfecting our own nature. God is putting us to the test: Do we deserve chocolate, or not? God knew women would rebel if He didn't coax us to hang in there, which is exactly why He penned this more-or-less sappy Scripture: "Love is patient, love is kind . . . it is not easily angered, it keeps no record of wrongs" (1 Corinthians 13:4–5). C'mon, God, You know us better than that!

Yes, my mother was right. Women really are the better, finer, and wiser of the two sexes. Intelligent, durable, loving, faithful, feminine, loyal, and with eyes in the backs of our heads—are these not but a few of the many wonderful qualities of women? "She is clothed with strength and dignity; she can laugh at the days to come" (Proverbs 31:25). God knew it would take a supremely compassionate spirit to cope with man's inferiority complex of having been made from dust.

God knew it would take a tolerant temperament to deal with the "PRFK10" disorder that compels men to gawk at beautiful women. He understood that it would take an extraordinarily forgiving soul to deal with man's inattentiveness—or that blender, or the set of new blue-enamel pans we got for Christmas. He also realized it would take patience so as to control our joy—and ourselves—over the new set of knives we got for our birthday! Yes, God knew that only a woman could deal with the oddities of men—as well as *all* the other shortcomings that resulted from being the "first cookie out of the oven."

But chocolate is chocolate, and God wants a return on His investment. God never said men were perfect, and He expects our help in improving them. Does God not say, "I will make a helper suitable for him" (Genesis 2:18)? God knows that women are men's best encouragers to make something of themselves while here on earth. This job He left to women, because we can do it. In fact, we're perfect for the job. Didn't God also say, "She speaks with wisdom, and faithful instruction is on her tongue" (Proverbs 31:26)?

Men are lucky. God lets them know it, too, when He says that a woman of "noble character . . . is worth far more than rubies" (Proverbs 31:10). This means that you are of great value to your man—he's lucky to have you! Yes, you. As God says, "Many women do noble things, but you surpass them all" (Proverbs 31:29). Thanks be to God for His infinite wisdom when, after taking one look at Adam and persisting in "surely I can do better than this," woman came into being. And so we help our men become better beings. Praise God for making us the "better, finer, and wiser" sex . . . and for giving us chocolate as a reward!

● ● ● Questions for Discussion:

1. Why do you think God created woman to be the superior of the two sexes?

2. What unique qualities do women have that help them cope better than men with all situations in life?

3. When your partner is doing something that is really annoying, do you call on God to see you through?

4. Do you pass God's test for learning to live with a man—or are you still trying to get it right?

● ● ● Scripture for Reflection: *I thank and praise you, O God of my fathers: You have given me wisdom and power, you have made known to me what we asked of you.* —Daniel 2:23

● ● ● Prayer for Today: *Dear God, help me to have strength and patience on those days when my mate irritates me. Remind me that I'm not perfect either, and give me the wisdom to overlook the minor annoyances that characterize any relationship. Thank You for the gift of love and companionship—and the capability to handle the many challenges we'll face together. Thank You for women friends, dear God. I do not know what I would do without them! And thank You for inventing chocolate—which also makes the journey sweeter.*

34

What Makes a Memory Special?

● ● ● Donna Schuller

As I get older, I sometimes find myself longing for those days in the kitchen, making cookies with my mom.

recently saw a TV commercial that brought back wonderful memories for me. Two little hands first appeared in front of the camera, and then, as the screen widened, it became obvious that they were molding and shaping cookie dough. The camera then panned out farther to show a little boy making cookies with his mother. At some point, the announcer's voice came on and said, "With Nestlé's Toll House, you're not just baking cookies; you're making memories." As I listened to this advertisement, my mind immediately zoomed back to my mother's kitchen where she and I made our own Nestlé's Toll House cookies when I was a little girl.

I treasured these times, because it would be just the two of us—Mom and me—together in our aprons, mixing up the cookie dough. Of course, not all of the unbaked dough made it into the oven! We'd sample quite a few of our little creations as we carefully spooned the delightful little clumps of chocolate pieces and walnuts onto the baking sheets, making sure that they were perfectly sized and uniformly spaced. I remember the succulent smell as the first soft, warm, freshly-baked cookie melted in my mouth.

The scent was so unmistakable that my mind still embraces it today as I sit and recall this memory.

Do you have a treasured memory you love to revisit over and over? It is amazing how the seemingly littlest things can be so memorable. As I look back on this memory of making cookies with my mom, I am reminded of the care and nurturing she showed me as a child. The time that she spent making cookies with me cannot be measured by anything tangible, but she created for me a happy memory of unconditional love and approval. My mother made me feel so loved and accepted just by the simple act of taking the time to bake cookies.

As women, we have daily opportunities to give our families memories that will always remind them of our love. Do you take the time to create memories with your family and friends? We are all so hurried and rushed these days, and it seems as though there is limited time to indulge in these presumably small and insignificant activities. Life gets filled with so many tasks and "to-do" items that it is difficult to even go out to lunch with a friend just for the sake of being together. But as I get older, I sometimes find myself longing for those days in the kitchen, making cookies with my mom, and I pray that I have done a good job making meaningful memories with my children.

When was the last time you made cookies with your kids? When was the last time you flew a kite, went rock hunting, took a hike, did a craft project, looked for cloud formations or constellations in the sky, or wrote a story together? If you're like most parents, you probably can't remember the last time you engaged in these activities—if you ever did! Make a commitment now to remedy the situation.

The next time you're tempted to go to the store, take the kids to the park instead. The next time you decide to stop for fast-food ice cream, go home and make homemade Popsicles! The next time you start to put a CD in your car stereo, make up a song with your children instead. And don't forget to include God in your memory making. Read Bible stories with your children. Better yet, put on a play about Noah's ark and invite the neighbors to your show. Make a "date" to take your junior high or high school child out to lunch. Rather than *always* going as a family, take one child at a time to a movie. Go shopping—without them suggesting it first. Just "appear" in your teen's room; then just sit there and talk about lighthearted things (don't always go there with a lecture on your mind). Yes, at first it will annoy them, but they'll eventually relax and open up to conversation. God tells us in Psalm 45:17, "I will perpetuate your memory through all generations." Talk with your children about who you want to pray for, and say your prayers together. When you step away from the rat race and take the time to do these things, your children will not only be making wonderful memories, but they'll be building a closer relationship with God. And you'll be creating special moments that will last forever.

● ● ● Questions for Discussion:

1. What is your favorite childhood memory?

2. What feelings does this memory bring to mind for you?

3. God wants to be part of your happy memories; how can you spend more time getting to know God?

4. What memorable activities would you like to do with your family?

● ● ● Scripture for Reflection: *The memory of the righteous will be a blessing.* —Proverbs 10:7

● ● ● Prayer for Today: *Dear Lord, thank You for the wonderful memories we can recall from our childhoods. Help us to become creators of great memories for others by recapturing the simpler pleasures of life. Teach us to share with others the wonderful blessings and promises that are found in the Bible. Help us to slow down, put our to-do lists aside, and treasure the time we spend with our loved ones and with You.*

35

What Going to the Grand Canyon Teaches

● ● ● Bettie B. Youngs

We head to the mountains and to the water's edge, and to see the great canyons and glorious sunsets, not to increase our self-esteem, but rather, to feast our eyes and quench our thirst for the splendor of God.

From the majestic mountains to the intricacies of exquisite blooms, Mother Nature does have a way of flaunting her beauty, doesn't she? Perhaps nothing expresses the "ahhh" of nature better than the poignant words of Edna St. Vincent Millay when she was gazing upon a flower in bloom: "God, I think thou hast outdone thyself!"

Nature—so good for body, mind, and soul! One of my favorite nature places is at Sedona, a colorful masterpiece of 350 million years of creation. It is truly a place of intoxicating splendor, from the spectacular majestic red rock sculptures to the panoramic sunsets and garnet-colored skies, where clouds float like tufts of cotton balls. Whenever my physical eyes need to feed my spiritual eyes, I head there. From the moment I arrive, I can just feel the peace edging out the stress and strain of too much time in my office, and in the airport—and, well, with too many *people*!

I was just in Sedona this past weekend. I checked into my log-cabin–style accommodations and immediately headed to the water's edge, the lovely tumbling waters of Oak Creek. I have a tendency to mostly travel at the speed of light, but not in Sedona. Sitting there feeding the ducks, I note the precise moment when the fuchsia sun drops below the horizon; when a sliver of moon winks itself into a violet sky; and then, when a full heaven of stars comes sliding into view. You really can sit still that long in Sedona, in a stillness that has a voice of its own—a voice, I might add, that is sweeter than the love and laughter of friends and more important than victories or defeats. Always I assign this incredible sense of serenity to God. Do you have a place like this, a place that infuses you with the incomparable supremacy of the great Creator?

Yes, the wonder and beauty of nature leaves us with a feeling of awe and tranquility, but it does more: in nature we are reunited with larger truths—we live in a world of creation, one where a universal energy permeates all living matter. What a shame if we don't grasp the importance of being in harmony with what is all around us.

But being filled with an appreciation for the wonder and beauty of nature is not about telling ourselves what a great and wondrous world we live in, but rather that this, too, is just a part of the fullness of God. As much as we'd like to honor nature for all the ways it makes us feel, we do not, in the words of John Piper, author of *Seeing and Savoring Jesus Christ* (Crossway Books, 2004) "go to the Grand Canyon to improve our self-esteem. The reason for wasting so much space on a universe to house a speck of humanity is to make a point about our Maker, not us."

He's right of course. We head to the mountains and to the water's edge, and to see the great canyons and glorious sunsets, not to feel good about ourselves, but rather to feast our eyes and quench our thirst for the splendor of our God. As Piper explains, "The physical eye is meant to say to the spiritual eye, 'Not this, but the Creator of this.'" It is God, rather than nature, that is the desire of our souls. The deepest longing of the human heart is to know and enjoy the glory of God. Perhaps God uses nature to draw us in. Ephesians 1:18 speaks of "the eyes of your hearts." But we are thirsty for the glory of God, not to quench our taste for being enamored. When the beauty of nature fills our eyes and thus feeds our hearts, it is the glory of God—not nature—that we feel. Mankind's yearning for nature is simply a desire to know God more fully. Praising our Father must surely follow.

● ● ● Questions for Discussion:

1. In what ways does your physical eye feed your "spiritual eye"?

2. Do you have a special nature place where you go when you need R & R? What is it that attracts you to this place?

3. In what way do you think that mankind's yearning for nature is a desire to know God more fully?

4. What does the phrase "When the beauty of nature fills our hearts, it is the glory of God we feel" mean to you?

● ● ● Scripture for Reflection: *Lift your eyes and look to the heavens: Who created all these? He who brings out the starry host one by one, and calls them each by name. Because of his great power and mighty strength, not one of them is missing.* —Isaiah 40:26

● ● ● Prayer for Today: *God, You have created such a beautiful world. Help us know the great truth behind Your creations. When our eyes admire a sunset or the fragile wings of a butterfly or the intricacies of a flower in bloom, may we acknowledge Your awesome hand at work and say, "Not this, but You, the Creator of this is who my heart is loving." Lord, we know that the deepest longing of the human heart is to know and enjoy the glory of You, our heavenly Father. Thank You for giving us the beauty of nature to help us turn our hearts toward You.*

36

Are You "Fine" with Things?

● ● ● Donna Schuller

Are you really "fine," or just masking your true feelings?

like to greet people with "Hi, how are you?" Most of the time, the response is "Fine." Sometimes I can see by that person's expression, though, that he or she doesn't really mean "fine." I'm tempted to ask, "Are you *really* 'fine'?" because I know that the person is masking his or her true feelings.

Do you ever say one thing when you're feeling another? I think women do this quite a bit. We often learn, from the time we're young, that we're more likely to be liked and accepted if we're "fine" with things, so we never venture to reveal if we feel differently. But being honest with our feelings is important to good health—mental, physical, and spiritual, as I learned from personal experience.

One of the most rewarding challenges I have had in my ministry was when I wrote and implemented a seven-week divorce-recovery workshop for kids. I first offered my program to a private Christian school but was told by the principal that this was too sensitive a subject to address on the school campus. I couldn't believe this response! I felt she was really saying, "Kids from

Christian homes don't have this issue—and if they do, the pain and anguish divorce creates is far too private a matter to let the kids talk about." But I also knew from my own childhood that many children, in part, blame themselves for their parents' divorce. Worse, all too often they never get an opportunity to talk about their feelings—but they must if they are to develop in normal ways and move forward in their lives in healthy ways. I know from experience that when kids don't get the help and support to talk about things so as to heal the wounds created, they carry the pain and baggage into adulthood. So I was not about to take no for an answer.

I turned to the public schools and fortunately there was immediate acceptance. I started the program with about twenty kids ranging in age from seven to eleven years old. As you'd expect, parents took notice: after the first session, I received a couple of desperate phone calls from parents asking if it was healthy to have kids talk about their emotions. Many were afraid that doing so might make the children's emotional states worse, that it might cause them to relive their pain. And, of course, some of the parents were worried about *their* lives, even "family secrets," being discussed. But I knew this workshop was necessary for the kids because the parents were often going through such trying times themselves that they couldn't adequately help their children through the confusion, pain, and abandonment they may well be feeling. So I reassured the parents and pressed on in my work with the kids.

Each week I came in with a hands-on project so the kids could learn to express their feelings. One day I came into the room wearing a paper bag over my head with a happy face drawn on the outside. "How am I feeling today?" I asked. "Happy," they responded. I then took the bag off and, with a big frown on my face, again asked them how I was feeling. "Upset!" they shouted. "Exactly," I said. "Do you sometimes put on a happy face even when you're feeling sad or really hurting?" And we began to talk about masking feelings and the price we pay for doing that, as well as how to reach out to get the help we need.

This lesson was a real success with the kids. And yet, there would be a lesson in it for me, as well. I was only five years old the first time my parents got divorced. My parents remarried when I was eight—and then separated again when I was eleven. To complicate matters even more, my father was killed in an automobile accident when I was just thirteen. Every year I got a year older—but so did the pain I carried inside from coping with such painful experiences at such a young age. Doing this program for the kids made me realize that not only had I not worked out the hurt and anger that had filled my heart for more than twenty-five years, but there were other issues I'd not worked through—including abandonment. And there was a good possibility that there were still other issues that I was not yet aware of.

Slowly but surely, some of these began to reveal themselves. For example, when I became a stepmother, I had no clue what kind of parent to be—the model of parenting I'd grown up with certainly wasn't one I wanted to emulate. But here I was, parenting my husband's two little children—kids I knew just might be suffering with the same painful feelings I had as a child—and I didn't know how to soothe their emotional spirits, much less fix the damage I could tell the divorce was serving up for them.

As I was helping the kids in my divorce-recovery program, not only did my old pains surface, but it became clear to me that I hadn't just conveniently outgrown them: they were still there, just hiding behind the curtains in my life—but leaping into center stage when it came to matters such as doubting myself or sabotaging my ability to be confident, loving, and outgoing. *Well, thanks—but no thanks,* I said to myself. *These pains from the past are destructive emotions that do nothing but rob me of being all I can be. I'm going to clean house on them.* And that's what I did. One thing led to another, and eventually, I sought counseling.

I had been running away from it all my life, because I was

always afraid that if I was honest with people, they might not like me. I might not get the love and approval I wanted. Others might not think of me as the strong and capable woman I wanted to be—and hoped I was projecting. By helping the kids process their feelings in my divorce-recovery program, I was able to learn more about myself and thus begin my journey toward wholeness and healing. It has made a world of difference.

If you say you're "fine" but you know it's not so, seek healing. Start by having a talk with God. Luckily, God always knows what we are feeling, and we can never hide our emotions from Him. Even on the days when we put on our "happy mask" despite the pain we feel inside, God knows us. He knows our joys and our deepest, darkest soul secrets. He wants to help us heal, as we learn in Psalm 107:19–20: "Then they cried to the LORD in their trouble, and he saved them from their distress. He sent forth his word and healed them; he rescued them from the grave." Ask God for His love and acceptance, and let Him lead you to the person who will help you explore your feelings.

Find a counselor, a pastor, a good friend to talk about how to begin this process. Even though you may at first be tentative—because it does take courage to lay old issues on the table and sort them through—it is very freeing. Sometimes it takes a while to figure things out, especially if you have been playing a role for so long that you're not even aware of it, or you're afraid that others will reject you if you tell it like it is. God will make your paths straight and direct you toward a productive and joyful future.

● ● ● Questions for Discussion:

1. Are you "fine"?

2. What secrets, pains, or other unfinished business are you harboring but would just as soon lay on the table and be done with?

3. Have you shared your feelings with God in prayer?

4. How can your relationship with God help you feel safer in sharing your feelings with others?

5. How can you use your experience of harboring secrets to help others seek healing for theirs?

● ● ● Scripture for Reflection: *Trust in the LORD with all your heart and lean not on your own understanding; in all your ways acknowledge him, and he will make your paths straight.* —Proverbs 3:5–6

● ● ● Prayer for Today: *Dear God, thank You for teaching us honesty and transparency by the power of Your Holy Spirit. Help us to become more real with our feelings and keep us safe in the knowledge that You will make our crooked paths straight. Please lead me to that person or place where I can find healing. Thank You for turning our past experiences into something productive and great in Your time.*

37

The "God Box"

● ● ● Bettie B. Youngs

May we never be so arrogant as to believe we bring about our own blessings

Not too long ago, I received in the mail a "Wish List" from Sister Patricia Cruise of Covenant House in Los Angeles (which is a twenty-four-hour-a-day, year-round facility for homeless boys and girls). Sister Cruise's wish list included: two econo-size boxes of laundry detergent; two cases of toilet paper; forty gallons of milk; five jumbo cans of soup; eighty loaves of bread; ten econo-packs of bar soap; fifteen jars of peanut butter; ten jars of jelly; one case of shampoo; and two large variety packs of first-aid strips. It looked like a reasonable request and a worthy cause to me, and I gladly sent a donation.

At a book signing the very next day in Chicago, I listened as former tennis star Andrea Jaeger described her wish list in her work with helping kids with cancer. Her list included: finding and renting an 18,000-square-foot facility that could house some 500 kids at a time; finding and training a dedicated staff to work with kids with cancer; community opportunities for a wide variety of enrichment activities, along with vehicles to transport ill children to and from these activities; an annual budget in the millions to support these and other goals; an IRS-confirmed 501c nonprofit status; and an affirmation from God to confirm her calling to help children with cancer. No small list, to say the least!

All this got me to thinking about how God asks His children to involve themselves with helping and supporting the good of His children. It also got me to thinking about my own immediate wish list. At the time, at the top of mine was: the continued deepening of faith; good health for my daughter and for myself; to acquire a rental property; staying committed to fitness goals and leisure time with friends; and a publishing contract for a new book. What's on your list? Take a moment and jot down your top five.

Formal or informal, articulated or just on our minds, we probably all have a wish/want/hope list. Maybe yours includes things such as a happier marriage or finding a special someone with whom you can share committed love. Maybe you're wishing to become a first-time parent or to improve the relationships you share with your children. Perchance you're wishing for more sleep or a peace-filled home. Or maybe you're hoping to find a good home for a pet you can no longer keep, or desiring to banish post-partum blues or menopause symptoms. Maybe you'd like a more fulfilling job, or to win the lottery—among other things. Always, always we humans are wanting, wishing, hoping for something. It's only natural. So answer the following: Whatever is on your wish list, do you think you'll get it? If so, when? How will the results show up? Finally, can you bring about your wish on your own, or will it take—literally—an act of God?

In a world that coaches us to be all we can be, have all we can get, and "climb every mountain," it can be easy to think *we* cause things to manifest on our own. *We need to wean ourselves of this notion.* It is God, not us, who fulfills our wish list. Do you believe that? Do you trust God implicitly to grant the desires of your heart? God *is* the granter of blessings. Certainly Sister Patricia Cruise and Andrea Yeager had the wisdom to turn to God in asking for what they needed. And each trusted God to bring it. You probably aren't surprised to learn that Sister Patricia's list was filled many times over (in just one day), and at year's end, Andrea Yeager's staggering list was not only fulfilled, but in ways that she could never have invented on her own.

How about you? When blessings—goals, desires, wishes, wants, whatever you call them—show up, do you think they've come to you by your own doing? Or, if you believe that all things show up via God, do you thank Him? In other words, do you count your blessings? But how can we thank God for the blessings He bestows unless we know how many wishes we've asked for—and know which ones He's granted?

Some years back, a friend told me about a "God Box," a wonderful way to understand the benevolent nature of God. Sometimes used by clergy and spiritual counselors, a God Box is simply a container—such as a box or a drawer—where you keep your stash of "Please, God, I need/want/wish/dream of . . ." Go ahead and try it. List all that you've asked of God this month, and place the wish in the drawer or box. And, yes, do label it "My God Box"! At the end of every month, and again on Christmas Day, take stock of all you've asked of God and all He's granted. By doing this, just as in having a to-do list, you can readily see all that has been granted—and in what ways. For example, my wish for a contract from a certain publisher to do a Christian inspiration book for teens was granted—but with modifications. God granted a publishing contract, but for a women's book (this one!) and with a publishing house that was even more suitable than the one I previously had in mind.

Yes, our Creator is a most benevolent Father, one who doesn't put a quota on the number of blessings we're each allowed. May we have the wisdom to trust that God provides as promised in Deuteronomy 28:2: "All these blessings will come upon you and accompany you if you obey the LORD your God." May we *never* be so arrogant as to believe we bring about our own blessings, but may we *always* remember to give glory to our heavenly Father for all that He provides.

● ● ● Questions for Discussion:

1. Do you "count your blessings"?

2. When good things happen, do you see them as luck, fate, or God's blessing?

3. Do you have a wish list? If so, do you keep track of how many of them come true?

4. Do you believe that the fulfillment of your wish list depends on your prayers, on tithing, or on something else?

5. Do you give God praise for all that He provides?

● ● ● Scripture for Reflection: *Look at the birds of the air; they do not sow or reap or store away in barns, and yet your heavenly Father feeds them. Are you not much more valuable than they? Who of you by worrying can add a single hour to his life?* —Matthew 6:26–27

● ● ● Prayer for Today: *God, thank You for Your awesome blessings. I praise You for all the wonderful blessings You have bestowed upon me. I am fast to thank You for the good that comes. Lord, please help me to see the love behind those blessings that do not turn out to my pleasing. Teach me to be patient, Lord! Oh, how many times I have seen that what I thought was a negative, turned out to be the best outcome for me. Teach me to trust Your wisdom, God, and to have faith that You will beam a spotlight on the path that is best and right for me.*

38

Have You Ever Had an Affair?

● ● ● LInda C. Fuller

When we place God at the center of our marriages, and not push Him to the side when "life" sets in, we can overcome whatever threatens to divide us.

Have you ever had an affair? I have. I can tell you from experience that it is a breach so severe that the trip back will teach you every nook and cranny of your heart!

Adultery can quickly break down, as well as break up, a marriage. No surprises there. Betrayal is such a hard blow when exposed. It takes a strong couple—and much prayer—to repair the damage done to vows that promise to faithfully love and cherish one another. Certainly the statistics show us that many, many couples are never able to make amends in ways that can repair and restore the trust and love that make a marriage work. But because of the healing power of forgiveness, adultery doesn't have to break up a marriage. If it did, my husband, Millard, and I would have been divorced after six years of marriage! But, as I put pen to paper, we just celebrated forty-five years together—good years filled with love, trust, and great purpose. Our marriage is stronger than it ever was. But that didn't happen overnight. Getting to where we are now took a huge amount of work—and would never have been possible without much prayer and forgiveness.

We started out like all young couples, in love and with all the expectations in the world of being together for a lifetime. Then reality struck: careers, kids, and goals consume a huge deal of time and energy. My husband's number one drive was to become financially successful. Like so many men of that generation, Millard believed financial success bought family happiness. He also thought that providing his family with money and the things that go with it—the big house, car, and extremely comfortable lifestyle—made him a good provider, and thus a good husband.

His drive to succeed was realized: he'd become very wealthy by literally working day and night, not to mention some weekends. And Millard wasn't the only one whose time was booked solid. Even though we started a family right away, I was equally driven to get my college education, which meant attending classes during the day and studying after the kids went to sleep at night. I was usually asleep by the time my husband got home from the office. For nearly five full years, our lives were booked solid; we lived a day-to-day rat race.

Little did either of us realize how our marriage would suffer if we didn't spend quality time together as a couple. But at the end of our sixth year of marriage, we were two people who, though married, were mostly passing each other coming and going. I was unhappy on so many levels but not sure how to change any of this. So I got "involved." My extramarital affair lasted for two full years.

You can only imagine the guilt and chaos I was feeling during this time. My marriage wasn't as fulfilling as I'd expected it to be, and now my emotions were being drained into yet another direction. Amazingly, during the time I was having an affair, I was teaching Sunday school and playing the organ at church. I knew our lives were off base and that the affair was all wrong, but I didn't know how to make a clean break.

After a great deal of agonizing over how to straighten out my life, and not wanting to spread our personal problems around the town where we lived, I left Millard and our two children and went to New York City to seek counseling from a pastor we knew. It was during my second week of counseling when a breakthrough happened: "If you loved each other once, you can love again," the counselor explained. And new hope was born for healing—for both my marriage and me.

While I was away learning how to begin again, my husband was experiencing a rebirth of his own. Now spending evenings with our two children, ages three and five, Millard had the responsibility to feed and bathe them and to read them stories and put them to bed. As he was tucking our son into bed one night, Chris looked up at him and said, "Daddy, it's great having you home!" This touched Millard very deeply. He never realized until then just how much the children had missed him—or what he had been missing by not being more involved in the day-to-day care of our children.

After two weeks apart, Millard and I met in the lobby of my hotel. He looked terrible: I had never seen him so distraught. We tried going to a movie at Radio City Music Hall, but left during intermission. We walked along Fifth Avenue and sat down on the steps of St. Patrick's Cathedral. I knew that the only way our relationship could ever have a new beginning was if I was completely honest with him about everything. I told him that even though we were married, I felt alone and lonely. I told him that having all the things that money could buy was convenient but didn't translate into my being truly happy. I told him how disappointed I was that he didn't want to see me and the children more.

And then I told him about my affair.

I did this with fear and trembling, because I really anticipated that he would just walk away forever. Instead he embraced me. Consumed by our grief, we both cried so hard that several people passing by even asked if we needed help. But that was the beginning of a new relationship and a commitment to re-create our lives so that we could once again honor our vows of marriage.

Almost immediately Millard began talking about selling his business and giving the excesses of our lives to charity . . . a bold and new beginning! I was amazed, because I thought he would never want to give up the successful business he had worked so hard to build. But the bigger change was the focus on our lives together and reestablishing, maybe even redefining, a relationship. Rebuilding trust didn't happen overnight either. It took time to recapture the closeness we had when we first married. And it took the better part of several years for us to put in place what God had led us to—the creation of Habitat for Humanity International, a nonprofit, worldwide ministry of providing decent and affordable homes for low-income families around the world.

God was faithful to us, allowing our hearts to open so as to make healing possible and to give us work that would provide a new purpose—His plan—for our lives.

Adultery is a very serious sin. Yes, we like to rename it "infidelity," but in the eyes of the Lord, it is adultery. Still, no sin is too big for God to forgive if there is true repentance. An adulterer must sincerely ask forgiveness from God and from his or her spouse for healing to begin. Do you remember the story of the adulterous woman in John 8? The townspeople brought a woman to Jesus who had committed adultery, and they reminded Him that Moses had commanded that such a woman be stoned. But Jesus had a different reaction to the woman's sin. First He told the crowd, "If any one of you is without sin, let him be the first to throw a stone at her" (v. 7). Realizing that none of them were without sin, the crowd left, leaving Jesus alone with the woman. He then said to her, "Woman, where are they? Has no one condemned you?" (v. 10). When she agreed that none had done so, Jesus replied, "Then neither do I condemn you . . . Go now and leave your life of sin" (v. 11).

Can you imagine the incredible relief this woman felt when Jesus showed her this amazing love? Jesus forgave the woman if she promised to commit adultery no more, and He offers the same forgiveness to us if we do the same. His wisdom offers direction on how to live righteous lives, as well as a way to wipe the slate clean and start over when we break down. Marriage doesn't necessarily need to break up when it breaks down. And when we place God at the center of our marriages, and not push Him to the side when "life" sets in, we can overcome whatever threatens to divide us in the first place.

● ● ● Questions for Discussion:

1. Has infidelity been the cause of a separation or divorce for you?

2. If you have committed adultery, how have you attempted to make amends?

3. Do you think it is possible to rebuild a marriage that has been broken down by adultery?

4. What conditions must be met for God to forgive the sin of adultery?

5. Do you think couples who put God at the center of their lives are assured of never having their marriage broken through adultery?

● ● ● Scripture for Reflection: *You shall not commit adultery.* —Exodus 20:14

● ● ● Prayer for Today: *Dear Lord, my husband and I have promised to love and cherish each other all the days of our lives. During those times when I feel neglected or unloved and am tempted to be unfaithful and break my marital vows, please help us to be able to communicate, that we might solve the problems in our marriage. Show us how to center our relationship around our love for You so that we may always live in Your grace. Teach us to love each other as You love us, for all eternity.*

39

Living Large

● ● ● Bettie B. Youngs

*If you've been afraid to share your love of God with those
around you, ask God to give you a greater love for them.*

Have you ever noticed how some people think they have to
apologize for talking about God? I recently taught a
weekend university extension course called Christian
Inspiration: Writing to Publish. Of the forty-five enrolled would-
be authors, many prefaced their comments with remarks such as
"I don't mean to offend anyone, but I see God as . . ." and then
proceeded to tell about the thesis of their work. I was amazed that
in a class advertised as "Christian Inspiration," folks thought they
had to apologize for the way they wished to glorify God in their
impending works or books.

That so many felt apologetic when publicly referring to God
reminded me of a time when I attended a gathering at the home
of good friends Denny and Barbara Metzler. Painted in elegant cal-
ligraphy above the door of their home is the Scripture "As for me
and my household, we will serve the LORD" (Joshua 24:15). Upon
entering their home that day, the person in front of me looked up
at the Scripture and—as though it didn't speak for itself—said to
her friend, "They're Christian." To this the woman's guest replied

(referring, I presume, to the words above the entrance), "Very gutsy!" Say what? What exactly is so gutsy about announcing to anyone entering your home that you are, in fact, entering a home wherein the people serve their Lord?

Unfortunately, even some who profess to be Christian aren't comfortable announcing their faith. I'm currently on a tour for my book *Living the 10 Commandments in New Times*. I'm friends with a number of professional speakers, some of whom sell my titles along with theirs from the back of the room at speaking events. One such person called to order fifty copies of an assortment of my titles. When I told her about the *10 Commandments* book, knowing that as a Christian she'd be thrilled to add this title to her sales, I was amazed to hear her say, "Oh, what an awesome book to have done! But I'll have to pass on it. I mean, inspiration is one thing, but I wouldn't want to offend anyone by offering a 'God' book."

Not everyone, of course, is afraid to speak out. There are those, like Jerry Stevens from Boca Raton, Florida, who five times a week (sometimes twice a day) takes to the skies in a yellow crop duster (named *Holy Smoke*) where he soars some 9,500 feet above Palm Beach County to pen "Love God" in white smoke. The messages, which span seven miles, can be seen forty to fifty miles away, often lingering in the clear-blue sky for fifteen minutes. "We're bombarded with so many messages that God's message is being crowded out. This is like a full-page ad that a whole city can see at the same time. It makes people happy," says Jerry. You go, Jerry! We don't all have to live our love this large for God, of course, but why are we so afraid to be bold for God? Are you? Are you willing to "live large" for God?

Jesus predicted that many of his followers would not be brave enough to publicly proclaim their faith. He foretold that Peter, a loving and loyal follower of Jesus, would deny knowing Him three times within one evening, which is exactly what happened. Why do you think some people are afraid to wear their hearts on their sleeves when it comes to God? What are we afraid of? Surely it cannot be for fear of being ridiculed by nonbelievers. As writer Melvin Graham chides, "Shame on me—shame on all of us—for all the opportunities we've had to be a good witness and to share Christ, and we didn't do it. It wasn't convenient, or we were a little embarrassed" (*Decision*, July–August 2004). If we wish to be a true disciple of Christ, worthy of being welcomed into eternity with God, we must be willing to live our faith. If you've been afraid to share the good news—the love of God—with those around you, ask God to give you a greater love for them. Speak out, and don't be afraid. God will give you the right words; this He has promised. Are you a believer? Truly a believer? Have the wisdom to live it openly.

● ● ● Questions for Discussion:

1. In what ways do you witness of your love for God?

2. What does it mean to live boldly for God?

3. Do you ask for God's blessings openly, such as at mealtimes in restaurants or at the homes of family and friends, or do you open business meetings with a prayer for God's guidance? If not, what would it take for you to love those around you enough to provide such leadership in demonstrating your love for your God?

4. Have you challenged others to run their lives—even their families and businesses—in a way that honors Christ?

● ● ● Scripture for Reflection: *I am not ashamed of the gospel, because it is the power of God for the salvation of everyone who believes.* —Romans 1:16

● ● ● Prayer for Today: *Thank You for the promise of Your Word, Father. I pray that I will trust You rather than lean on my own understanding. Thank You for the promise that says when we trust in You, we will become like a tree planted by the waters, that spreads out its roots* by the river. It does not fear, and it always bears fruit. I pray that I will be a tree of Your planting, Lord. Lead me to drink freely of Your waters of life. Fill me with Your Holy Spirit so that I might have the courage to speak boldly and publicly of my love for You. With Jesus and His apostles as my models, help me to spread Your good news by my words and my actions.

40

Left Behind!

● ● ● Donna Schuller

When your day is nonstop, wall-to-wall busy, do you say,
"God, You'll have to wait until later," or do you say, "God,
please be with me every step of the way today"?

A friend of mine left work one day, stopped by the store to get groceries, and then hurried home. It wasn't until she was putting the groceries away that she realized she'd forgotten to pick up her child from school! (She hurried back to get the kid, of course.) Another friend once told me that she was in such a hurry buying groceries that she was almost out of the parking lot before she remembered she'd left her twelve-year-old browsing in the store's video department (and, yes, she returned to fetch her daughter!). We laugh (after the fact) at such bloopers, of course, but such experiences are probably tell-tale signs that we women have a lot on our minds and shoulder a lot of responsibility (and are always in a hurry). So it's not surprising that we forget something or someone, every now and then.

I remember a time when I was a part of a group, and someone almost got left behind. I was in Africa with my family, along with Ken and Pat Behring, founders of the Wheelchair Foundation (a nonprofit organization that distributes wheelchairs anywhere in the world to those in need). Ken and Pat had graciously invited my husband and our family to join them on a twelve-country trip while delivering wheelchairs on behalf of their foundation.

One day, by mistake, we almost left Pat in Kinshasa, Congo. The error happened when we'd all lined up to use the restrooms before boarding the plane. I guess no one noticed that Pat was still in the restroom when the government official (who was carrying our passports) whisked the fifteen of us through the gate to the tarmac and on to the jet. Once on board, we were all busy settling in, and I guess we just forgot to do a head count! About ten or fifteen minutes later, as we awaited our departure, we saw Pat being let on to the plane! Can you believe we almost left her behind? (And it was her own private jet!) We were beyond embarrassed, of course, and aghast that we'd almost left her. But here she was, coming down the aisle, remarking calmly (and, no doubt, tongue in cheek), "Gee, I guess you guys forgot about me!"

Not that it wasn't an ordeal for her: a government official was not about to let her leave the country without her passport—which we had on the plane. All Pat could do was point in the direction of the tarmac where her jet was sitting. It took about fifteen minutes for her to convince them that she should be on our plane where, of course, they found her passport and realized she was telling the truth.

As these examples demonstrate, it's easy to leave people behind when we get caught up in what we're doing or are in a rush. Do we sometimes get so caught up in our lives that we leave God behind?

When your life is nonstop, wall-to-wall busy, do you say, "God, You'll have to wait until later," or do you say, "God, my day is nonstop, so I want to ask for Your blessings throughout the day, and I want to ask if You'll be with me every step of the way today"?

Take a moment to think about this and how important it is that we not forget to make God the center of all we do. Go ahead and take stock. Do you jump right into your day without asking for God's blessings and guidance first? Do you leave Him at church on Sunday when you go about the rest of your week? Do you forget to consult God before you make a major decision? Do you embark on a trip without seeking His protection? Do you let your child go out for the evening without praying for his or her safety?

God wants to be the most important part of our day. Matthew 6:33 tells us, "But seek first his kingdom and his righteousness, and all these things will be given to you as well." God never forgets us. No matter how busy your life becomes, make sure that in everything you do, God doesn't get left behind!

● ● ● Questions for Discussion:

1. Is your relationship with God a hit-and-miss one?

2. How does starting (and ending) your day with God in prayer enrich your life?

3. What is the single most important thing you can do to put God first in your life?

4. What is the most important thing you can do to not live life "on a treadmill"?

● ● ● Scripture for Reflection: *Be careful that you do not forget the Lord.* —Deuteronomy 6:12

● ● ● Prayer for Today: *Dear God, forgive me when I forget to include You in all that I do. I never want to leave You behind as I embark on my busy day. Help me to become more like Your Son, Jesus, by teaching me to ask for Your help and guidance at all times, for You are the most important part of my life.*

41

Does God Have a "Play Mode"?

●　●　● Bettie B. Youngs

God knows that the best way to have playtime with me is to catch me in my garden.

Do you think God has a "play mode"? I do. Experience tells me it's one of His greatest personae. I truly believe He loves to play with His children, using whatever means He can. In my case, I think God knows that the best way to have playtime with me is to catch me in my garden.

I love the early morning hours. And I especially love to be in my garden this time of day. So my early morning ritual is to walk through the yard with a glass of juice in one hand and my clipping shears, to cut fresh blooms for the day, in the other. Even my flowers are happy at this time of day: certain ones seem to call to me, "I'm colorful and beautiful; let me sit on your desk today!" So I snip a bloom here and a bud there and, of course, remove a weed here and there. And, yes, I talk to my flowers! I'm not beyond telling you that my vocabulary in the garden is often reduced (or should I say, "elevated"?) to phrases such as "Ooooh, so beautiful!"; "Oh, so lovely"; "Wow—totally awesome!"; "Amazing!"; or "Simply stunning!"

My sense is that God is watching and smiling at the fact that

I'm thoroughly amazed and amused by the glorious color and intricacies of His flower creations. I mean, have you ever seen a blue passion vine in bloom? How about a red one, or its cousin, the purple one? Well, I have all three! I first learned of this glorious vine when visiting a friend, Sally Wright, in Toronto. So taken with the vines' splendid blooms, I knew I needed to have them grace a particular wall on the west side of my house. When you see a passion vine in bloom, you are certain that God is boasting about the artistry within Him!

And so in the garden, I clip blooms to come inside for the day, all the while smiling and often literally teasing God, saying things such as "All righty then, God, there is nothing timid about Your flower power here." Or, "Wow! That's a little arrogant, isn't it, God?" Or, "I'd like to know what was on Your mind when You created this one, God!" I know that because my blooming garden is an ear-to-ear smile for me this also brings great pleasure to God. I open my doors in the early morning hours to walk into my yard, and my first words are "OK, God, what have You got for me today?" I know He hears and is present.

But God doesn't stop playing with me just because I see His newly bloomed creations. Invariably there will be a plant that looks a little sad because another taller one in front of her stole her drink of water from the late-night water sprinkler, so I offer it a splash. Like magic out of nowhere, a hummingbird or two comes swooping down to play, diving in and out, in and out of the spray of the water. This, too, brings me great delight, so I seize the moment to interact with them. I spray the water high into the air to let the hummingbirds bathe in it. And in these moments my heart is so light and filled with the love of God. Always I say, "God, You know how to bring delight to my heart." When I step back into my house, I've had a thorough dose of joy and fun. And God knows it.

Recently, my daughter was visiting and spent the night. Up early the next morning (a rarity for her), she had stepped into the yard and was quietly observing God and me in "play mode."

When I saw her watching, I told her how I had experienced this time and time again, and how I always assigned this special time for communing with God. "I'm not surprised," she offered. "God plays with me too. When I was little, He played with me through my pets, especially those two little white kittens we had when we lived in the condo. And He was always very present when I spent time with my horse, Brockton. He's played with me on a million occasions, and He still does. As a matter of fact, it happened again yesterday. As you know, I have a similar daily ritual of starting my day by walking in my yard, looking at the flowers, just breathing the fresh air in and out and thanking God for a new day. But yesterday I awoke in a really bad mood. Perplexed and annoyed by this feeling, I couldn't quite find a reason for it. I stepped into my yard, simply standing there for a minute. Suddenly, a bird called out in a strange caw, over and over. It was a boisterous and weird sound, and I could do nothing but laugh. Then the bird's call turned to a more pronounced "hello, hello, hello." Taken aback, I was by now just totally focused on the bird. Then in that same moment, the bird flew away. Immediately my thought was, *God will do anything to love His children. He knows I'm in a bad mood and saying, 'I don't think so!'* He was totally playing with me! And you know, without that goofy caw from the bird, my bad mood might have continued throughout the day. But the bird totally distracted me and transformed my mood. I lifted my arms heavenward and said, 'God, You are amazing! Thank you!' And Mom, the rest of the day was just awesome! It was a 'God day,' no doubt about it!"

Do you ever feel as if God "plays" with you? It's a delightful thought, one you must allow yourself—because it brings you closer to God. Our heavenly Father is a God who wants our hearts to know and feel love. My mother said it this way in a poem she penned on the inside of her Bible:

WE MAKE HIS LOVE TOO NARROW, BY FALSE LIMITS OF OUR OWN.
WE MAGNIFY HIS STRICTNESS WITH A ZEAL HE WOULD NOT OWN.

IF OUR LOVE WERE BUT MORE SIMPLE, IF WE TOOK HIM AT HIS WORD,
THEN OUR LIVES WOULD BE LESS COMPLICATED AND WE'D KNOW
THE PLAYFULNESS OF OUR LORD.

How true. Children seem to instinctively know when God is playing with them. They laugh when they fall into a mud puddle, the cat tumbles into the bathwater, or they sneeze in their soup.

Allow God to bring joy and laughter and light into your life. Delight in the Lord! The Bible teaches us to find pleasure and joy in all that God has created for us. "Let the heavens rejoice, let the earth be glad; let the sea resound, and all that is in it; let the fields be jubilant, and everything in them. Then all the trees of the forest will sing for joy" (Psalm 96:11–12). God made the beauty of the earth and all its creatures that we might feel happiness in their presence. Be willing to see God's playfulness in your life. "This is the day the LORD has made; let us rejoice and be glad in it" (Psalm 118:24).

● ● ● Questions for Discussion:

1. Do you think God has a sense of humor?

2. In what way has God shown you His "play mode"?

3. For what reasons do you suppose God uses humor in our lives?

4. Have you ever prayed for more joy and laughter in your life?

5. How does loving the Lord result in an instant joy in one's heart?

● ● ● Scripture for Reflection: *He will yet fill your mouth with laughter and your lips with shouts of joy.* —Job 8:21

● ● ● Prayer for Today: *God, help me to always recognize those times when You are beside me, wanting me to lighten up. Thank You for brightening my days and adding joy, fun, and playfulness to my life. Thank You for using this humor to remind me that You love me so much that You are willing to come out and play. Remind me to do that more often.*

42

Imaginary Bears

● ● ● Donna Schuller

Women, especially, are vulnerable to imaginary bears.

Several years ago I went camping in Yosemite, California, with my daughter and her eighth-grade class. During our precamping briefing, we learned that Yosemite National Park has an abundance of bears. The principal of the school spent a good part of two hours explaining how important it was that we have no sweets in our tents, not even scented lip gloss or deodorant. The bears might smell these items and break into the tents in pursuit of them. He assured us that we would have plenty of room to store our food products and cosmetics, because all campsites are equipped with "bear boxes," which are very large, solid-steel containers that are securely fastened with two steel bars.

As we set out, the girls talked and talked about the trip, but none of the conversation was as rich as the discussion about avoiding the bears. By the time we arrived at the campsite, the young teens had entertained many possible scenarios regarding possible bear attacks. We were more than convinced that we needed to follow all directions so that we could avoid inviting one of these unwanted creatures into our tents.

The first night was relatively uneventful, with the exception of the cold temperature that dipped into the twenties. It was June, and everyone had assumed that it would be much warmer. The second night held a different surprise: I had been asleep in my one-person pup tent when I was awakened by a very peculiar noise. It seemed as though something was outside and was gently rubbing on the outer surface of my tent. This noise increased in both its intensity and frequency on both sides of my tent. About that time, I heard some very loud and hysterical cries coming from the tent next to me, where one of the female teachers was staying. She was screaming, "Help!" over and over, and then she yelled out my name, "Donna!"

At that moment I remember praying and asking God to give me wisdom and guidance in this situation. Part of me wanted to simply ignore her; I certainly didn't want to get eaten by a bear! The other part of me was saying, "Get up and help this woman!" I finally gathered up enough courage to slowly part the nylon of my tent and peek outside. What I saw was absolutely amazing. About six inches of fresh snow blanketed the ground: what I had been hearing was the snow as it hit the top of the tent and gently slid down the side, growing louder as the amount of snowfall increased. As I looked around the campsite, I could barely see some of the other tents that had been so expertly pitched hours earlier. They now looked like miniature toy tents, and several seemed close to completely collapsing from the weight of the snow.

The teacher who had called for me was still screaming at the top of her lungs. As I gathered my composure, I called out to her, "Don't worry; it's not a bear. It's snowing!" Once she realized she was not in danger, she pulled herself together, and we both started laughing hysterically. As you can imagine, it took quite a while for our adrenaline to stop pumping so we could finally try to fall back to sleep. We sat up for some time as we rehashed the situation and the ridiculous events that had led us to the point where we thought we were being attacked by bears.

Have you ever been the victim of an "imaginary bear"? We frequently create imaginary bears in our lives when we let our fears of "what if" paralyze us from taking positive steps. Do you create imaginary bears in your relationship with God? For example, are you afraid to return to church after a long hiatus, thinking everyone will stare at you and politely tell you what a heathen you've been? Or is the bear in your head? You think, *Well, I'd like to be a regular churchgoer, but everyone in the congregation will scrutinize my every move, and I won't be able to go to Las Vegas anymore.* Oh, yes, there are plenty of bears to go around, as Proverbs 23:33 warns: "Your eyes will see strange sights and your mind imagine confusing things." But imaginary bears are not as benign as they may seem. They can separate us from a loving God, from knowing God.

As women, we seem to be especially vulnerable to fears of the unknown. *What if my child gets hit by a car while walking to the store? What if we get robbed while out jogging? What if I paint my house the color I really want and the neighbors don't like it?* Our concerns about what others might think can keep us from venturing into unknown territory. But Jesus assures us in Matthew 6:34, "Therefore do not worry about tomorrow, for tomorrow will worry about itself." If we refrain from jumping to illogical conclusions and cast our fears aside, we will have a better chance of separating fact from fantasy and be able to enjoy the many blessings of God in this wonderful adventure called life.

Don't let your imaginary bears prevent you from building a closer relationship with God or from doing anything else that will add richness to your life.

● ● ● Questions for Discussion:

1. Do your fears prevent you from doing things that will enrich your life?

2. Have you been afraid to build a closer relationship with God because it might place too many restrictions on you or put you under scrutiny?

3. How does God want us to treat these imaginary bears?

4. What imaginary bear would you like to cast aside today in order to venture into unknown territory?

● ● ● Scripture for Reflection: *Now we see but a poor reflection as in a mirror; then we shall see face to face. Now I know in part; then I shall know fully, even as I am fully known.* —1 Corinthians 13:12

● ● ● Prayer for Today: *Dear Lord, sometimes we jump to unreasonable conclusions that prevent us from drawing closer to You. We also let our fears of the unknown keep us from enjoying the many adventures that await us in life. Help us to separate fantasy from reality and not to worry about what might happen or what others might think. Teach us to open our eyes so that we may see things as You see them.*

43

Traveling Light

● ● ● Bettie B. Youngs

We depart this earth with the single possession with which we came: our soul.

When we enter our Father's kingdom, all that each of us will be able to bring is our very souls. Never did I understand this more clearly than the day we children laid my father to rest. The six of us had agreed to make any and all final plans together. You can imagine our surprise—and disbelief—when, as we began the procession to the cemetery after the service, the hearse turned onto our country road and headed to my father's farm instead of going directly to the cemetery. My older sister and I, who were in the head car, thought the driver didn't know the way to the cemetery and told him to turn back. But the driver informed us that our younger brother had authorized a last-minute pass around our dad's homestead.

As we slowly passed the farm that day, there was the proof that at the end of our lives we leave without anything we have accumulated here on earth. Gazing at the yard of the homestead, there sat the twelve-foot-long wooden picnic table our father had lovingly built to accommodate his large family and their spouses, children, and grandchildren. Oh, the joy we had when we gathered around that table! Near the table sat Dad's beloved collie, watching the Canadian geese Dad so affectionately called to and fed every day. There was his beautiful new truck, decked out in all the ways he wanted it, and all the farm equipment—serious tools for the greatest and most meticulous farmer there ever was. Shed after shed—the huge one housing many expensive machines, all bought and paid for with the honest sweat of his brow. There were other sheds too, dilapidated ones he hadn't repaired, because in the later years of his life, he wasn't sure if that was the best use of "good" money.

I looked to the family home, where I'd dwelled nearly every day of my childhood years, and recalled the large and busy family who had lived and loved therein. I was so grateful that this beloved father of mine had so loved and honored my mother and had found their relationship worthy of his willful and great devotion.

But seeing the wilted flowers on the deck and knowing that next to those flowerpots was where my father shed his boots each evening—but no longer—I knew this part of our family's life was over. I felt so sorry for myself and for my other brothers and sisters for our loss of our parents, and so very sad for my little brother, who was so obviously overwhelmed by the enormity of his great loss that he made this decision to have our daddy travel one more time past the life he knew and so loved. Still, for all that Dad had achieved—which was remarkable given that he had an impoverished beginning but had worked hard to finally achieve a life of comfort—none of that mattered now. Dad had journeyed on, stepping out of this world and into the house of his Lord with the same single possession with which he'd begun his journey here: his soul. Not even my beloved father—my staunchest friend and most trusted confidant, the brightest and most handsome man I'd ever known, someone I knew to have *all* the answers—could escape this great truth.

● ● ● Questions for Discussion:

1. What have been the most important possessions you've accumulated?

2. Does God discourage us from acquiring earthly possessions while journeying on earth?

3. When your days on earth are over and others look at the life you've led and the possessions you've accumulated, what will they learn about the value you assigned to living—and dying?

● ● ● Scripture for Reflection: *Naked a man comes from his mother's womb, and as he comes, so he departs. He takes nothing from his labor that he can carry in his hand.* —Ecclesiastes 5:15

● ● ● Prayer for Today: *God, thank You for the greatest and most prized possession of all—our souls. For all that we acquire during our lifetimes, we know that it is only temporary, and that our abundance is to be used to assist our brothers and sisters the world over to experience the joy of life. We are so greedy, Lord. Forgive us for this. Please help us to see that, as much meaning as we attach to things we acquire here on earth, they are merely things, meant only for this world. Show us how to instead build up our spiritual lives so that we might be prepared to spend eternity with You.*

44

It's Time to Think About *ME* . . . for a Change!

● ● ● Linda C. Fuller

I've finally figured out that "overwhelm" means it's time for me to take care of me.

Have you ever gone through a time when life seemed overwhelming? It's happened to me! While some people may have the idea that I am Supermom or Wonder Woman, I can do only so much! I have learned the hard way that when I start to feel overwhelmed, it's time to make adjustments—in relationships or tasks or whatever else is pulling me down, pushing me up against the wall, boxing me in—you get the idea. So, I've finally figured out that "overwhelm" means it's time for me to take care of me.

It takes a lot to break me down, but when something does, I need R & R—big-time. I remember several years ago when I was overly consumed with work and travel, and I wasn't taking care of myself. I got to the point at which I couldn't sleep, didn't enjoy the foods I usually do, and wasn't motivated to do much of anything except lie on the sofa. This state was so unlike anything I'd ever experienced that I called my doctor, who told me I had the classic symptoms of clinical depression. Fortunately, he referred me to a good psychiatrist, who prescribed antidepressants, a daily walk, and talk therapy. But aside from helping me balance out my bloodstream, she explained how I got this way: my stressful lifestyle was making me sick!

I discovered while going through this that it's really difficult to talk about. I mean, who wants to hear for the third time "I'll pass on that; I'm just not feeling myself today," or "I'm just so *down*"? I wasn't exactly the positive go-getter I'd always been, and even I'd have to admit I wasn't that much fun to be around. "Feeling down"—for the umpteenth time—is not going to get you much sympathy, either. In fact, I learned there is much negative stigma surrounding "feeling down" (especially for illnesses like depression). It's no wonder that women try to mask it—or self-medicate as much as they do. But suffering through tough times is one thing; going through them alone is even worse.

I guess the good news is that these times can be opportunities to ask how we can lead more pleasurable lives. And this is exactly what God intends for His children to have: abundantly joy-filled lives. And so we must ask how we can do this. For one woman, it may be to make more time in her busy life to play with her children or grandchildren. For another, it might mean living in a recreational vehicle at a Habitat for Humanity site for several weeks to help families build themselves a home. "Whatever melts your butter" is what you should do, a wise friend of mine suggests. I would add, however, that it should also be whatever God is calling you to do. But in doing for others, we must also remember to take care of ourselves. This is what God wants us to do, as Paul reminds us in 1 Corinthians 6:19: "Do you not know that your body is a temple of the Holy Spirit, who is in you, whom you have received from God?"

The mind and body are interdependent, so you must care for your physical self and do those things that bring relaxation and fun to your life, as well. As I began to apply all this common wisdom, I had to admit that for many years I had wanted a pet, but I did not get one because I traveled so much. I knew it wouldn't have been fair to the pet to be alone or cared for by someone else.

Finally, having decided that it would be in my best interest and God's call on my life to stay home more, I jumped at the chance when I saw some cute kittens old enough to leave their mother. I had been advised to get two so they could be companions. Well, those little kittens have brought so much joy into my life—and surprisingly, to my husband, too. They cuddle with us on the sofa at night and play hide-and-seek and jump under the covers when we are *attempting* to make the bed in the mornings. As I've discovered, pets can amuse us, de-stress us, and add lots of love to our lives. My point is, don't put off doing those things that bring love and laughter to your life. Having a couple of cats may seem like more responsibility to you, but the delight they bring into my heart is immeasurable.

If you know you need to take some time for yourself, do it. Women are great at taking care of others' needs—but often at the expense of their own. Taking care of yourself is not a selfish thing to do; it is a way of loving others, because you are making sure that you can be there for them—and to be there with a happy heart! I once read a quote by former Texas governor Ann W. Richards that went, "The most important thing you can ever give another person is to be a happy and healthy person." What areas of your life are you neglecting? Think about these four areas of your life, and ask yourself some tough and honest questions:

Spiritual: Do I need to spend more one-on-one time with God? Do I need to take more private, quiet time for reading the Bible and inspirational works? Do I spend the time I want in prayer?

Physical: Am I in good health? Am I eating well and exercising? Do I need to join a gym and get fit? Should I take a yoga class or do more walking? Are my annual medical exams up-to-date? When was the last time I had a complete physical?

Emotional: Am I as happy as I'd like to be? Am I spending time alone, away from family and work responsibilities? Do I have effective skills to manage the stress and pressure of life? Am I making the time I want to do the things that interest me—such as gardening, painting, or writing?

Social: Am I nourishing friendships and social ties? Do I want to spend more time with women friends? Do I need to visit or call my parents or children more? Do my husband and I need to spend more—or less—time together?

Of course, you will want to add other pertinent questions, but you get the idea. The goal is to take inventory to see if you are caring for yourself in all the ways you should—especially at those times when it feels that life is pulling you down, pushing you up against a wall or boxing you in.

You're worth it, of course, but know that God wants you to care for yourself, too. "I pray that you may enjoy good health and that all may go well with you, even as your soul is getting along well" (3 John 2). Nurture yourself so that you might give praise to the Father: "You restored me to health and let me live" (Isaiah 38:16). Healthy mind, healthy body, healthy soul, healthy relationship with God . . . now, that's the way to take good care of yourself!

● ● ● Questions for Discussion:

1. Have you ever been sick because you tried to do too much for others and ignored your own needs?

2. Why do women often feel guilty about caring for themselves?

3. Why does God want us to care for ourselves as we care for others?

4. Have you reevaluated your life lately and prayed about what you could do to take better care of yourself?

● ● ● Scripture for Reflection: *Exercise is good for your body, but religion helps you in every way. It promises life now and forever.* —1 Timothy 4:8–9 CEV

● ● ● **Prayer for Today:** *Heavenly Father, sometimes I feel overwhelmed by life—as if I'm being pulled in a hundred different directions and never finding time for myself. Please teach me to slow down and to pay attention to my own needs. Help me not to feel guilty about caring for myself. Show me the best way to nourish my mind, body, and soul so that I can be the person You created me to be. With all my heart, I want to thank You for caring about me and loving me just as I am.*

45

"So, What Do You Do?"

● ● ● Bettie B. Youngs

*Why would we assign a bigger "ooh" to the discovery of a
cancer cure than the raising and training of a little soul?*

Have you noticed how much status we assign to someone
in a career or role we deem important? When I mention
that I'm a writer, for example, ears perk up. "Wow!" comes
the response, followed by a hundred and one questions. If I say,
"Right now I'm taking a little time off work to spend more time
with my family," practically no one wants to hear more! This
same reaction is elicited during group meetings or dinner parties
when the following question is addressed to the people in the
room: "So, what do you do?" These days you can usually count
on some very impressive answers: "I'm president of the World
Bank of London, Tokyo, and the Virgin Islands." "The company I
founded supplies food to 3 billion starving children on four
continents." "I'm responsible for $5.9 trillion in assets with Smith,
White, Collier, and Lundgren." These answers are greeted with
oohs and aahs.

Invariably, though, someone is there who has chosen to be a
stay-at-home parent or who has stepped off the corporate ladder
and into the demands of full-time parenthood, at least temporar-

ily. When that person admits, "I'm home raising children," the reaction is usually, "Oh . . . but what do you do other than that?" Only someone who has never been home raising a family will ask this, of course.

My friend Susan Heim recently gave up an exciting career in publishing to stay at home with her newborn twins. She has two other children, as well. With twin babies, she knows the meaning of work—and fatigue. She recently shared this with me:

> One twin's a night person; the other's a day person. At midnight, one baby is asleep; the other is wide awake! Just as we settle down our little night owl at the crack of dawn, the other twin is ready for his feeding. Both babies sleep wonderfully when they're being held, but as soon as they're set down, they suddenly wake up! Although I know this stage in my babies' lives won't last forever, it sure seems never-ending when I'm awakened five times a night. But I love it and wouldn't trade it for the world.
>
> I miss my career in publishing, but I'm so busy in my life as a mother and wife that quite honestly I couldn't do both—at least not right now. Nothing could be more important than raising my family. If ever I doubt this, I need only listen to how my prayers have changed. While I've always asked God to give me the strength to persevere when I'm tired and to help me not to get cranky when I haven't slept well, I also used to pray about things like getting a book finished in time for a major appearance or for the self-control to not blow up at some executive within the company when he made a decision I didn't agree with.
>
> Now I still pray about sleep, but only as it relates to my children, such as, "Lord, thank You for this precious child I hold in my arms at three in the morning. There's

nothing I'd rather be doing than rocking this gift to sleep." And whenever I think I can't handle things any longer, I ask myself: *Which is really more precious to me— being a mother* (albeit an exhausted one!) *or getting eight hours of sleep?* Put in those simple terms, the answer is obvious. I wouldn't trade my little ones for any amount of sleep! I thank God that my sleeplessness is not from worry or stress, but rather from the wonderful gift of having these children.

Why would we assign a bigger "ooh" to the discovery of a cancer cure than the raising and training of a little soul? Consider Susan's work as the full-time parent of four children. Her job affects the lives of each family member in her home, as well as their functioning as they go about their day. And it will affect generation after generation of people in her family—and the world, as well. Maybe it's because such jobs fall into the category my mother used to call "No one knows what you do unless you don't do it." Why do we fail to see the importance of such roles? It's like filling bags with sand to save a town from flooding. There's nothing glamorous about filling bags with sand, but saving the town is something else altogether. Saving a town gives meaning and purpose to the drudgery of filling bags with sand.

Do you ever feel that what you do is unimportant? Feeling this way is not exclusive to stay-at-home mothers. There are many other jobs that don't appear to be glamorous or that are done more or less behind the scenes. This does not take away from their value. In fact, if you check the Bible, you'll find that hardly anyone was revered for being a great politician, ruler, or corporate executive. Many of the apostles were simple fishermen. Joseph was a humble carpenter. Mary, the most important woman in the Bible, is given great respect merely due to her loving role as Jesus' mother. Although these people were considered unimportant to most of society, God clearly felt they were of utmost significance to humankind. This same lesson can be applied to our own stations in life: as long as what we do is for the purpose of serving God—and you believe that caring for His children is high on His list—it is of vital importance.

● ● ● Questions for Discussion:

1. Have you ever felt that what you do for a living is unimportant?

2. If so, how did you realize (or have you?) that in God's eyes, it is absolutely of great importance?

3. How does your job or career benefit the lives of those around you?

4. How can you convince yourself that what you do is hugely important in the overall scheme of your life—and God's plan for your life?

5. How can women support each other—in private and public— in allowing us to focus on what is best and right for us, without feeling that what we're doing doesn't measure up to what someone else may be doing?

● ● ● Scripture for Reflection: *Just as each of us has one body with many members, and these members do not all have the same function, so in Christ we who are many form one body, and each member belongs to all the others. We have different gifts, according to the grace given us.* —Romans 12:4–6

● ● ● Prayer for Today: *God, I may not be an important person in the eyes of the world, but I know that I will always be important to You. Help me to see that what I do is of value and is equally worthwhile as what others do. Thank You for the talents and gifts You have given me that I may do my job—whatever it may be—in a way that is pleasing to You.*

46

Will Someone Please Remind Me Why I Married This Guy?

● ● ● Donna Schuller

Have you ever asked yourself, "Why, exactly, did I ever marry this guy?"

Have you ever been so mad or fed up with the man in your life that you said to yourself, "Why, exactly, did I ever marry this guy?" If you are a normal woman who is completely honest with herself, then you have to admit that there have been times when you have asked yourself this question. I know I have! And it's not the just the big things; sometimes even the little things can be annoying! I mean, sometimes just the way my husband brushes his teeth or turns out the lights at night really bugs me. Men! I am not above admitting that while I have been married nearly twenty-one years, adore my husband, and think he is the greatest guy in the world, there are times when I feel totally disconnected from him and wonder why, exactly, I married him in the first place!

Having vented—at least a little—I'll also tell you that when I begin to feel taken for granted or negative about my husband (which are sometimes one and the same), it is usually a warning sign that the stress and pressures of everyday living are beginning to take their toll, because we have not spent enough "alone time" together. Can you relate?

It's pretty easy for couples to get so wrapped up in making a living, managing the kids, running errands, and taking care of all the other various projects going on, that we unconsciously neglect the "us" in the relationship. I know that at times in our relationship, I feel like nothing more than a business partner—I am the manager and head taskmaster of the running of our home and attending to the million-and-one needs of growing children, as well as being in charge of a thousand other things (that probably no one really knows I do unless I *don't* do them).

Do you ever feel that way—that because you are attending to the many responsibilities of normal everyday life, apathy and frustration set in? I do, and I don't like it one bit!

The thing is, I don't want to *not* have a dynamic relationship with my husband. But I know it can happen. So over the years, I've discovered that I need to creatively find ways to keep my marriage fresh, fun, and interesting. I know you know what I'm talking about! So at those times when I sense that my marriage is losing its vitality, when my heart yearns for that feeling of being in love all over again, I let my husband know it's time for some one-on-one time together. Believe it or not, men really aim to please, and they are fairly easy to figure out.

As for my husband, he's a very smart guy, so when I let him know I'm frustrated, he tunes in. He's learned from experience that when I say, "Let's talk," he should say "okay." At these times, my husband and I set aside time to just be alone together. We try to make it face-to-face time, as opposed to sitting in a theater seeing a movie. The goal is uninterrupted time to talk and to be close.

Do you do this? Spending time together may be as simple as taking walks together, pulling the plug on the television, or talking at the table after dinner. You don't have to spend a lot of money—surprising your husband with a picnic dinner and taking it to the beach or to the park at sunset is a great, affordable thing to do. When my kids were younger, I even hired a college student to help them with their homework so I could sit quietly for a while with my husband.

I'm not suggesting that you don't build an evening around "doing things," because that's good too. Anything that makes you feel that you're growing together is good, such as an evening shared with a Bible study group, followed by dinner out. Or maybe it's time to move "learn to dance" from your to-do list to your calendar.

Another important thing is to honor special occasions, especially your wedding anniversary. Don't get stuck in taking-you-for-granted mentality, thinking it is not important to buy your husband a card or write him a note of appreciation. All of these things help to preserve what is special between you. If you have the opportunity, go away for the big anniversaries. Robert and I recently went away to a very romantic spot for our twentieth wedding anniversary, spending four nights on Little Palm Island, a most beautiful little isle in the Florida Keys. There were no telephones or TVs! After we got over the withdrawal of not having the news every night, we settled in and once again learned to appreciate the special qualities that attracted us to each other in the first place. I got away from the tasks of cooking and cleaning, and Robert got away from his responsibility of acting general contractor on our home-remodeling project. And both of us got away from the responsibilities of parenting, as well as our ministry and work outside of the home.

As for the "manager of kids" role, you sometimes need a break from this job, as well. I can't imagine one woman not admitting that for all the joy and fulfillment our children are, raising kids is a huge source of stress for couples. Although children are a wonderful blessing in a marriage, somehow in the process of becoming a family, married people often lose the feeling of being close, even lovers. As endearing as it may be to call each other "Mom" and "Dad," it is not such a good idea, because we start to forget that we are also "husband" and "wife." Even on date nights, it's natural for the conversation to revolve around the care and needs of our children.

Raising children consumes much time and energy, but it is still crucial to reserve some of it to focus on each other. Don't feel guilty that you're not including the children in all your plans. Your time alone can actually benefit your kids. Experts say that couples with strong marriages make better parents. The peace and love that couples feel from a successful relationship spill over to the entire family, benefiting everyone. You are not neglecting your children's needs by taking some time away from them; consider that it is one way you look out for you so that you can look out for them.

God expects us to be happy in our relationships. We read in Ephesians 5:33 that "each one of you also must love his wife as he loves himself, and the wife must respect her husband." So do those things that keep your love alive. Renew those little words that mean everything: "I love you," "I appreciate you," "I need you," "Thank you," "I'm sorry," and "You look really nice." There is much wisdom in making sure you do not neglect the "lovers" part of your relationship.

God intended marriage to be the core of a happy family. Ask God to help you find ways to continue to grow in your love for your partner. Pray for your husband, and pray for your marriage. When you do these things, you'll find it much easier to find the answer when you ask yourself, "Why, exactly, did I ever marry this guy?!" You'll know that it's because God intended for you to be together, which is why you are managing all that you do, because goodness knows he could never live without your love and help, as we learn in Genesis 2:18: "The LORD God said, 'It is not good for the man to be alone. I will make a helper suitable for him'"!

● ● ● Questions for Discussion:

1. What things about your husband annoy you—and how can you let him know in a way that will lead to positive change?

2. When was the last time you and your spouse spent time alone as a couple?

3. What would you like to do on your next date together?

4. In what ways has being a parent changed your marriage?

5. In what ways do you make God part of your couple's time?

● ● ● Scripture for Reflection: *Let love and faithfulness never leave you; bind them around your neck, write them on the tablet of your heart. Then you will win favor and a good name in the sight of God and man.* —Proverbs 3:3–4

● ● ● Prayer for Today: *Dear God, thank You for bringing this man of mine into my life. Sometimes I don't understand him, Lord, and we certainly don't always see eye to eye. But I know that we were meant to be together, and with Your help I'm certain our marriage can succeed. May we always make togetherness a high priority in our marriage. Help us to find time to be alone together so that we may remember the reasons You led us to each other in the first place. May our marriage be a blessing to our entire family and a reflection of our relationship with You.*

About the Authors

 Bettie B. Youngs, Ph.D., Ed.D., is the Pulitzer Prize–nominated author of thirty-two books translated into twenty-four languages. Dr. Youngs is former Teacher of the Year; university professor of graduate school education; and director of Instruction and Professional Development, Inc. Bettie has frequently appeared on *The Good Morning Show*; *NBC Nightly News*; CNN, and *Oprah*. *USA Today, the Washington Post, US News & World Report; Working Woman, Family Circle, Parents, Redbook, McCalls, Better Homes & Gardens, Woman's Day*, and *Time* have all recognized her work.

Her acclaimed books include *Living the 10 Commandments in NEW Times*; *A Teen's Guide to Christian Living: Practical Answers to Tough Questions About God and Faith*; *12 Months of Faith: A Devotional Journal for Teens*, and the award-winning *Taste Berries for Teens* series (fourteen self-help books for teens, including *A Teen's Guide to Living Drug Free*; *A Teen's Guide to Managing the Stress & Pressures of Life*; and *Taste Berries for Teens: Inspirational Short Stories and Encouragement on Life, Love, Friendship and Tough Issues*.) Other titles include *Safeguarding Your Teenager from the Dragons of Life*; *Taste-Berry Tales: Stories to Lift the Spirit, Fill the Heart and Feed the Soul*; and *Gifts of the Heart: Stories That Celebrate Life's Defining*

Moments. Dr. Youngs is the author of a number of videocassette programs and is the coauthor of the nationally acclaimed Parents on Board, a video-based training program to help schools and parents work together to increase student achievement.

Though her earlier work focused predominantly on the areas of education and developmental psychology, in recent years she is best known for her series of loving and beautiful short story books, works that clearly, familiarly, and warmly elucidate the human spirit, captivating the American psyche and winning her wide-range appeal with audiences young and old alike. Bettie serves on the boards of a number of organizations and is the recipient of numerous service awards for her contribution to community activities. Her daughter, Jennifer, is coauthor of the Taste Berries for Teens series. To contact Bettie, write to Bettie B. Youngs at 3060 Racetrack View Drive, Suites 101–103, Del Mar, CA 92014, or at www.BettieYoungs.com or www.tasteberriesforteens.com.

 ● ● ● Linda Caldwell Fuller is cofounder (with her husband, Millard) of The Fuller Center for Housing, as well as Habitat for Humanity International, the world's leading not-for-profit builder of family-owned homes, providing low-income families with opportunities to afford housing. Linda has played a leading role in encouraging and providing opportunities for women and mental-health advocates to participate in constructing Habitat homes. Along with Millard, she stays at the cutting edge of Habitat's rapidly expanding development with the completion of a milestone 200,000 homes for a million people in 2005.

Deeply involved in the betterment of her local community, she has received the Harry S. Truman Public Service Award, in addition to many other awards. She is coauthor of *The Excitement Is Building* and editor of Habitat's Partners in the Kitchen cookbook series and *Down Home Humor.* Linda holds a BS in elementary edu-cation from Huntingdon College (Montgomery, Alabama), and is the recipient of eight honorary doctorate degrees. She and Millard have raised four children and have eight grandchildren.

To contact Linda, write to Linda Fuller at The Fuller Center for Housing, 701 S. Martin Luther King Blvd., Americus, GA 31719, or www.fullercenter.org.

● ● ● Donna Schuller is a certified nutri-tional consultant and the wife of Robert A. Schuller II, a minister at Crystal Cathedral in Garden Grove, California. She completed a program in General Family Services with an emphasis on drug and alcohol treatment and recovery at Saddleback College and earned a degree in natural health and nutrition from Trinity College of Natural Health. Donna has worked extensively in the field of human services. She imple-mented a divorce recovery program for elementary-school chil-dren; is an active participant in the Possibility Living ministry, where she teaches nutritional workshops for adults and children.

Donna also works closely with her husband in their international ministry and is author of *A Legacy of Success . . . Building Hope for Tomorrow.* She serves as the vice-president of Soroptimist International of Laguna Beach and is the recipient of the Woman of Distinction award for volunteerism in her community. She is also on the board of trustees for Schoolpower of the Laguna Beach schools. Donna lives in Laguna Beach, California, with her husband and two chil-dren. To contact her, write Donna Schuller, c/o Pat Nye, Crystal Cathedral, 12141 Lewis Street, Garden Grove, CA 92840, or go to www.dschuller.meta-ehealth.com or www.posliving.net.

Acknowledgments

We would like to thank the many people whose lives are written into the very fabric of this book. First, our publisher, Thomas Nelson, for giving wings to this book and for seeing it off to the hearts and hands of our readers. A really special thanks to Jonathan Merkh, first for his good fortune in finding such a "dream team" to write this book (!) and second, for his considerable wisdom in publishing it! We do thank you; your charm and playfulness have so added to our joy in accomplishing this heartfelt work. And to the other wonderful staff at Thomas Nelson, especially Editor Kristen Parrish—your expertise is so evident throughout—thank you; and a special thanks to Kathleen Crow for knowing the answer to every question we asked, and for always tracking down Jonathan when needed—we know how difficult that must be!

● ● ● Words from Bettie: I'd like to thank my awesome co-authors on this book, Linda Fuller and Donna Schuller. Years and years ago, Linda encouraged me to do a Habitat for Humanity Women's Build with her along with a really great group of women builders in Palm Desert, California. This eventually led to the First Ladies Build in the Appalachian Mountains, an incredible experience where some thirty-two Governors' wives and two former U.S. Presidents' wives worked side-by-side in the building of a Habitat for Humanity home for a family in need. I went away from these experiences with calluses on my hands, but with a heart full of love and respect for this truly magnificent woman and the Christian ministry that builds more than houses and touches lives around the world, as will Linda's newly founded The Fuller Center for Housing.

And to Donna Schuller, whom I first met years ago at a Renaissance Weekend. I saw a beautiful, six-foot-tall woman who, like a gazelle, entered the room with such grace, style, and confidence that I knew I wanted to know this glorious being! Thank you, Donna, for all the fun we had in doing this book. It is truly amazing what you've done, given that your computer is in the garage, your desk is in the hall, and you have no floor in your office. When your remodeling is done, we *are* going to party!

Thank you to my soul mate of a child, my beloved daughter, Jennifer. She *is* the wisest woman I know! Nothing has taught me the importance of prayer more than knowing that her life, and my guidance and interdependence thereof, are a destined ledger for which I will have to answer.

Thank you, dear friend and my "best sister," Susan Heim, for your consistently excellent work. Susan served as editor on some of my other titles at another publishing house, and when she left her day job to care for her newborn twins, we both knew we wanted to remain friends and find a way to work together—and this book afforded that opportunity. When she sent me a card that said, "Thank you for bringing me closer to Christ," I realized we'd shared the most profound gift one friend can give another.

I've never liked the phrase "labor of love" because it sounds, well, odd. But that is exactly what this collection of devotionals is. There is nothing more wonderful for me than doing work that takes me deeper into the heart of God's love, and this book has done that. It has been soothing, healing, and growing. Thank you, my heavenly Father.

● ● ● Words from Linda: For many years I have worked alongside my husband, Millard, writing books related to the ministry of Habitat for Humanity International. I've also edited Habitat cookbooks and a humor book that are sold to raise money for building Habitat homes and support The Fuller Center for Housing. Because of the dynamic and goal-driven man I married and the four outstanding children with which we have been blessed, my life is full to the brim, now more than ever, with interesting experiences, travel, and more and bigger challenges. We have had disappointments and personal crises like everyone else, but through them we learned how to persevere and even prevail. Most of all, we credit God for leading us to places where His love and helping hands are needed most.

Woman to Woman Wisdom has been one of those challenges that has given me the privilege and opportunity to share rich memories and spiritual encounters. I have never had the pleasure of collaborating with women who share so much in common with me concerning life and the Christian faith. Bettie and I have known each other for more years than either of us would like to admit. I have read a number of her books and have long admired her. So when she invited me to coauthor a women's devotional book, I was truly honored and excited about the prospect. And Donna, through this book I have come to know you in a very special way, and look forward to spending time with you and Bettie as we respond to the life this book creates. Writing it has been a delightful and insightful journey: We three women have been straightforward and unrestrained with each other as we wrote, edited, and expressed what we *really* think. Also, the search for suitable Scriptures has been a valuable exercise in reflection and self-examination as I put words on paper. Most importantly, I praise God and give Him the glory for whatever good comes from these universal and very relevant stories, Scriptures, and prayers for these times.

● ● ● Words from Donna: This book was a laborious task for me, to say the least. I still have a couple of active teenagers at home, and I never have enough time to get through my already busy schedule of serving a worldwide ministry and maintaining my practice as a nutritionist. So when Bettie asked me to co-author this book, I just didn't see how I could add one more thing to my to-do list. But I knew this was an important project and that God wanted me to have the faith I could do it.

The Bible tells us in Hebrews 11:1 (NASB) that "faith is the assurance of things hoped for, the conviction of things not seen." My hope for you, dear reader, is that you will have faith and believe that God has a wonderful plan for your life. With His help, you can grow beyond what you ever thought you could! God is truly faithful.

I want to thank my mother whose many talents I have grown to appreciate more every day. She had to be both mom and dad to my brother and me growing up, and I have grown to understand how difficult it must have been for her. (My hat goes off to all you single moms!) I also want to thank my husband, Robert, who has taught me what it means to love unconditionally. He has been my rock through many challenges, including the writing of this book. And, finally, to my coauthors: Bettie, with her commitment to her work with women and their families, and her diligence and dedication in writing about things that really matter. And Linda, it's been an honor for me to cowrite with you, such a hard-working woman who has given back so much to the world by helping to supply one of the basic needs of humanity—affordable housing. You are both awesome and inspiring!

● ● ● And from the three of us: As always, thank you heavenly Father for the gift of life, the joy of the journey, and the promise of life everlasting.

—Bettie B. Youngs, Linda C. Fuller, and Donna M. Schuller

Other Books by the Authors

Books by Bettie B. Youngs, Ph.D., Ed.D.

Gifts of the Heart: Stories That Celebrate Life's Defining Moments (Health Communications, Inc.)

Taste-Berry Tales: Stories to Lift the Spirit, Fill the Heart and Feed the Soul (Health Communications, Inc.)

Living the 10 Commandments in New Times (Faith Communications)

A Teen's Guide to Christian Living: Practical Answers to Tough Questions About God and Faith (Faith Communications)

12 Months of Faith: A Devotional Journal for Teens (Faith Communications)

Taste Berries for Teens: Inspirational Short Stories and Encouragement on Life, Love, Friendship and Tough Issues (Health Communications, Inc.)

More Taste Berries for Teens: A Second Collection of Inspirational Short Stories and Encouragement on Life, Love, Friendship and Tough Issues (Health Communications, Inc.)

A Teen's Guide to Living Drug-Free (Health Communications, Inc.)

Taste Berries for Teens #3: Inspirational Stories and Encouragement on Life, Love, Friends and the Face in the Mirror (Health Communications, Inc.)

Taste Berries for Teens #4: Inspirational Stories and Encouragement on Being Cool, Caring and Courageous (Health Communications, Inc.)

365 Days of Taste-Berry Inspiration for Teens (Health Communications, Inc.)

Helping Your Child Succeed in School (Active Parenting)

Getting Back Together: Repairing the Love in Your Life [Second edition] (Adams Media)

Safeguarding Your Teenager from the Dragons of Life: A Guide to the Adolescent Years (Health Communications, Inc.)

A Taste-Berry Teen's Guide to Setting & Achieving Goals (Health
  Communications, Inc.)
A Taste-Berry Teen's Guide to Managing the Stress and Pressures of Life
  (Health Communications, Inc.)
*Taste Berries for Teens Journal: My Thoughts on Life, Love and
  Making a Difference* (Health Communications, Inc.)
*Stress & Your Child: Helping Kids Cope with the Strains & Pressures
  of Life* (Random House)

Books by Linda C. Fuller

The Excitement Is Building (Word, Inc.), coauthored with
  Millard D. Fuller.
Partners in the Kitchen Cookbooks (Favorite Recipes Press,
  Inc.), a series of three cookbooks: *From Our House to Yours,
  Home Sweet Habitat,* and *Simple Decent Cooking.*
Down Home Humor (Favorite Recipes Press, Inc.)

Books by Donna Schuller

A Legacy of Success: Building Hope for Tomorrow (J. Countryman)